contents

SUMMER 2016

columns

short fiction

features

photos by Patricia Rustin-Christen

photo by Patricia Rustin-Christen

SUMMER 2016

saddlebag DISPATCHES

volume 2 • number 2

www.saddlebagdispatches.com

staff

Dusty Richards, *editor-in-chief*

Gil Miller, *managing editor*

George "Clay" Mitchell, *features editor*

Patricia Rustin-Christen, *photographer*

Casey W. Cowan, *art director*

Richard Howk, *marketing director*

Sophia Murray, *webmaster*

contributors

Rod Miller • J.B. Hogan

John T. Biggs • John J. Dwyer

Velda Brotherton • Linda Broday

Darrel Sparkman • JC Crumpton

Gordon Bonnet • Pamela Foster

Terry Alexander • Predator Black

Chet Dixon • Richard Prosch

Patricia Rustin-Christen

Prix Gautney

advertising

*For advertising rates and
information, please contact:*

*Dusty Richards, Editor-in-Chief
dusty@saddlebagdispatches.com
or
479.304.8562*

*For art guidelines and
ad submissions, please contact:*

*Casey W. Cowan, Art Director
casey@oghmacreative.net*

GALWAY PRESS

saddlebag DISPATCHES

WHERE STORIES OF THE WEST COME TO BE TOLD

Submission Guidelines

Galway Press is Oghma Creative Media's western imprint, and *Saddlebag Dispatches* is our quarterly e-magazine. We are looking for short stories, serial novels, poetry, and non-fiction articles about the west. These will have themes of open country, unforgiving nature, struggles to survive and settle the land, freedom from authority, cooperation with fellow adventurers, and other experiences that human beings encounter in the frontier. Traditional westerns are set left of the Mississippi River and between the end of the American Civil War and the turn of the twentieth century. But the western is not limited to that time. The essence, though, is openness and struggle. These are happening now as much as they were in the years gone by.

Query letter: In the first paragraph, give the title of the work, and specify whether it is fiction, poetry, or non-fiction. If the latter, give the subject. The second paragraph should be a biography under two hundred words.

Manuscript formatting: All documents must be in Times New Roman, twelve-point font, double spaced, with one inch margins all around. Do not include extra space between paragraphs. Do not write in all caps, and avoid excessive use of italics, bold, and exclamation marks. Files must be in .docx format. Submit the entire and complete fiction or poetry manuscript. We will consider proposals for non-fiction articles.

Other attachments: Please also submit a picture of yourself and any pictures related to your manuscript.

Manuscripts will be edited for grammar and spelling.

Submit to submissions@saddlebagdispatches.com.

Put *Saddlebag* in the subject line.

BEST OF THE WEST

A BRIDE FOR GIL
ISBN: 978-1-63373-045-8

THE MUSTANGER AND THE LADY
ISBN: 978-1-63373-083-0

SPIRIT TRAIL
ISBN: 978-1-63373-129-5

AND COMING SUMMER 2016...

GALWAYPRESS

hang tight,
COWBOY

Dusty Richards
editor-in-chief

Well the Ranch Boss—as they call me these days—has been busy since we last met here. *A Bride for Gil*, the first in my Brandiron Series, was recently featured on BookBub as a free ebook download for a week. Guess how many picked up a free copy? 40,000! No, you didn't read that wrong. If you're one of those number who gave me a chance, thank you so much. If you missed it, though, the book is still for sale in both ebook or print form on Amazon, iBooks, and Barnes & Noble. I also received notice recently that *A Bride for Gil* is one of the finalists being considered for the Western Fictioneers Peacemaker Award for Best Western Novel of the year. Getting western books out in the current book market isn't easy. Dwindling bookstore shelves along with the expense of distribution and returns makes it a tough business.

Next up for me is *The Texas Badge*, coming out in e-book, hardcover, and paperback in June. It's the third book in the Brandiron Series, and tells the story of a tough Texas sheriff who has to solve the biggest case of his career after a bank robbery, a jailbreak, and some bloody murders turn his little ranching town upside down.

But things don't stop there. In September watch for the next book in The Brandiron, *The Cherokee Strip*. Norm Thompson gets in a fight in an Ogallala, Nebraska alley over a man beating on a woman. Then his life takes a turn he never expected. On his trip home he discovers the Texas Cattlemen's Organization is leasing the Cherokee Strip—some call the Cherokee Outlet—to cattle grazers. But Norm must solve a rustler and a vengeance problem in Texas as well, and deal with the bad actors he runs into while grazing thousands of cattle on the Strip. This is the same ground years later that will be swarmed by the Sooner Boomers in a flight to get "free farms."

Last but not least, my rodeo book *The Natural* is now available, as well. It's an exciting story about a pro rodeo announcer and a rookie bull rider. The book is a re-publish, but many people missed it first time around. Rodeo folks thought it was great, though, so if you like rodeo, you'll be sure to enjoy it.

Coming up in late June, I'll be in Cheyenne, Wyoming for Western Writers of America's Annual Convention June 21 to 25. I'll be glad to meet you if you're there. Galway Press and *Saddlebag Dispatches* will have a table in the lobby set up, and I should be available around there during most days.

During my thirty years as a member of WWA I have struck up some great friendships. Many are gone on to a better place now. Jory Sherman, who handed me a membership form for WWA in February 1985 in Branson, Missouri. Elmer Kelton. one of the kindest, most generous, men I've ever met, and craftsmen at writing the west. Dick House, who in 1985 didn't have the postage money to mail the WWA newsletter, *The Roundup*, and asked me to help him set up an auction to raise money to. Robert Conley, my late Cherokee friend, who stopped me leaving the Cowboy Hall of Fame and asked me to be his WWA vice president. The list goes on and on of great writers who generously helped me climb the steps in the game of writing westerns.

There were setbacks in that climb. Rejections, falling outs, publishers that quit the western line. But western books are America's history, of the frontier that Thomas Jefferson bought in the Louisiana Purchase and adjoining land acquired later. Westerns tell the story of that land and the people who settled it. Jefferson didn't know about California gold and how the American people would spread out and civilize the land west of the Mississippi River. How after the Civil War we'd eat up all the hogs and chickens in the land, and Texas wild cattle would be on the butcher shelves as beef became a staple across the land. Why, he said it would be the year 2000 before we filled in all that land.

In this issue of *Saddlebag Dispatches*, we feature the National Chuckwagon Racing Championship held at the Bar ōF

Ranch in Clinton, Arkansas. You'll meet Dan and Peggy Eoff and their bunch—anyone who has 8,000 horses checked in for Coggins vaccination papers at the gates has to be one of the largest horse events in the world. I co-announced this event for fifteen years with Danny Newland, one of the greatest rodeo announcers in history. There's not a more exciting or dangerous event than wagon racing, and all the greats go there to compete. Bring your lawn chair, sit on the bluff, and watch the greatest event on earth spill across the Little Red River bottoms. The races are held Friday, Saturday, and Sunday afternoons Labor Day weekend and are proceeded by a week of Western and equestrian clinics and events.

This particular article would not have been possible, though, without the help of photographer Patty Rustin-Christen, owner of Porch Pig Productions, LLC. Patty travels the country shooting sporting events like this one, and gave us full acess to her galleries for use in this issue. She's a class act, and a helluva talent, to boot. So talented, in fact, that we've asked her to sign on as our official *Saddlebag Dispatches* photographer, and she has graciously accepted. Look for more of her work in our upcoming issues. You'll be as awed by it as we were—I guarantee it.

That's not all we've got for you in this issue, though. There's a beautiful photo tour of Eureka, California from my good friend and fellow author Pamela Foster, tracing her family's long and varied history with this funky little town on the edge of Redwood Country. We also have four new columns dealing with Western history and culture from the likes of Chet Dixon, John J. Dwyer, Darrel Sparkman, and Terry Alexander. Next issue, we'll be joined by none other than *New York Times* bestselling Western Historical Romance author Linda Broday.

If it's fiction you're looking for, don't miss the conclusion of JC Crumpton's powerful two-part short story, *Field of Strong Men*, Gordon Bonnet's *I Know What You Are*, J.B. Hogan's *Jailbreak*, John T. Biggs' *Sky Stone*, Velda Brotherton's *One Last Image*, and Predator Black's gritty *The Cochetopa Kid*. In the Fall, we'll be presenting an entirely new brand of Western fiction with the serial debut of *bender*, a graphic novel written and illustrated by Micheal and David Frizell.

I hope you enjoy the hard work of my cohorts Casey Cowan, Gil Miller, George "Clay" Mitchell, and the crew who have built this magazine from nothing. They make it all work, and we hope you sign up as a regular subscriber. Still wondering why we're not charging you to read such a quality work? Because we're dedicated to Westerns and Western writers. Every quarter we'll bring you some history, fiction, and spreads about people who promote and write the west as they see it. We want to bring back the western, and this is our way of doing it.

beyond the
TRAILHEAD

Chet Dixon
saddlebag poet

Every year beginning in September an insatiable urge awakens within me like clockwork. It's a call of the western high country. It begs me to pack my truck and hit the road to a trailhead leading into wilderness mountains. When I arrive at the trailhead I park my truck, grab my pack and head up the trail. While there are many destinations, the one normally chosen is timberline. Nothing compares to the magic you find there.

This love affair I have with the wilderness areas of the world began while on a hunting trip to the San Juan Mountains of Colorado when I was in my twenties. With inadequate equipment, food, clothing and knowledge, my brother and I hiked ten miles until we reached the base of Sheep Draw. We made camp at nine thousand feet elevation. Timberline was still 3,500 feet above us. Since we began the hike during a rainstorm in falling temperatures, we arrived wet and cold, with icicles hanging to our packs. On that hike, we learned how difficult it is to walk that far on a muddy packhorse trail. But we were young and energetic and didn't question the wisdom of our decisions. Regardless of how unprepared we were, that trip greatly impacted my life. It not only led to many trips since, it strongly inspired my writing, especially poetry.

My hunting and hiking expeditions through the western states created the inspiration for my recently-published book poetry, *Beyond the Trailhead*. The power that mountains give to my writing is difficult to explain, but deeply felt and life-changing. It never ceases to amaze me at how the wilderness and mountains only welcome you on their terms. At the same time, you feel free and independent and able to move beyond self-imposed borders of your life caused by rules, beliefs, values, practices and fears. It allows creative thought to flourish. It always makes poetry a perfect means of expression.

Any time I hike the valley pack trails or the interconnecting game trails criss-crossing mountain slopes, I feel a strong spiritual bond with nature. At these times, I am inspired to ask others to join me and experience the serenity and anger found in wilderness high country as well as its healing spirit. There is nothing quite as magical as beyond the trailhead.

Along a Road

When I stopped along a road today
To sit and rest a while,
Instead of hurrying on,

I knew that on ahead were other gems
To catch my mind and soul
But not like here alone.

Beside a weeping willow grove
Framing a rippling pool and mill,
I felt a sense of bliss.

I looked closely, listened well,
Knowing the little time I spend
Would be a time I'd never miss.

Now I look closely every time
At every stopping place
To find its value to share.

And when my life has lost control
I stop along some road and sit
Until it takes the weight I bear.

—*Chet Dixon is a businessman, philanthropist, and published author of multiple works, including the recently-published collection of poetry that shares its name with this column. He resides in near Branson, Missouri, but his heart lives in the western wilderness.*

Richards Opens a New Ranch

Dusty Richards is an author who goes right for the heart of the story, and *A Bride for Gil* is no exception.

Gil Slatter is the jinglebob boss for the TXY Ranch in Texas, but gets a promotion when the ranch foreman, Hank Thorpe, dies in the saddle of a heart attack just as they're about to start their spring roundup.

Once the roundup's over, Gil pays a visit to Hank's daughter Kate, who asked he come by when they were at the funeral. When he arrives, he finds she's set her cap for him. Impressed by her preparations, he accepts her proposal that she be his wife, even though he doesn't find her particularly attractive at first.

But while Kate may lack some in looks, she more than makes up for it in enthusiasm, wooing Gil quickly into married life. Their honeymoon is a trip to Fort Sill to buy horses, and Kate quickly proves herself as able as any man when outlaws attack their camp one night. Helping Gil hold them off, she has no qualms about carting the bodies to the nearest town marshal.

As he did in *Texas Blood Feud*, Dusty shows us the operative word in the term working ranch is the word 'working.' Running the TXY makes a lot of work for Gil, but he's willing to take it all on. He has the skills to do it, though. Grimes has full faith in him, faith that only increases over the course of this short but fully satisfying novel. The ranch's fortunes are on the upswing, and Grimes knows who's responsible for that: Gil Slatter.

But it's not all ranch work. There are bad guys aplenty here, too. Men like Kiley Masters, the spoiled son of a rich rancher. Kiley makes the mistake of drawing on Gil and finds out just how fast the ranch foreman is, causing a mess of trouble. On top off all that, Gil has to teach Kate how to dance, and then get her to dance in public with him.

Told with Dusty's usual lean directness, *A Bride for Gil* may have only one fault: that it won't be long enough to satisfy his many loyal fans.

—*Predator Black*
Author of The Cochetopa Kid

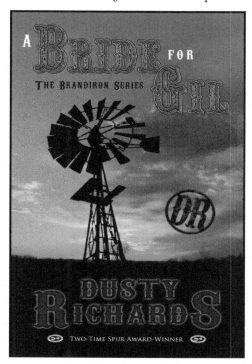

Crownover Delivers in Taut *Triple Play*

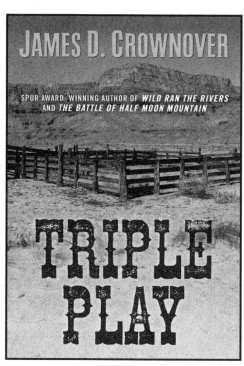

Once you start a journey, you can never predict how it will end until you get there. In *Triple Play*, a sweeping saga set in the desert southwest, James D. Crownover's authentic home-spun characters and dialogue will draw you into the compelling tale of Tucker Beavers and ranch life in general. Reminiscent of *The Searchers*, produced by John Ford, the journey of revenge turns into a quest for survival and redemption in the desert, with a cast of supporting characters you won't want to miss.

When the young cowboy's idyllic life is shattered by the death of his father at the hands of rustlers, he shoulders a man's duties and must put thoughts of revenge aside while the work of the ranch goes on. Finally, leaving his love and family behind, he hits the trail to bring his fathers' killers to justice and try and recover all the cattle that were stolen. The twists and turns of his story, including earthquakes, storms and shootouts, combine to bring the reader to the journeys end, savoring every word. Shocking. Poignant. Unexpected. The conclusion will leave you in wonder. Oh... and baseball.

A must read from the Spur Award winning author, James D. Crownover.

—*Darrel Sparkman*
Author of Spirit Trail

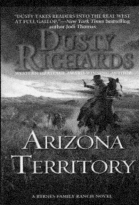
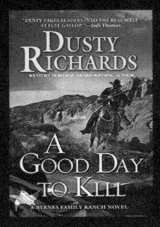
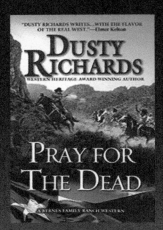
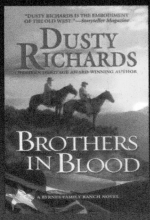

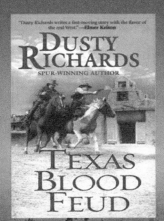
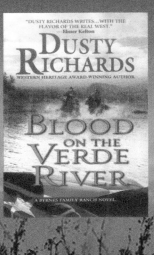
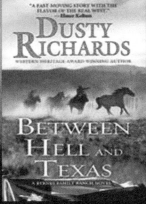
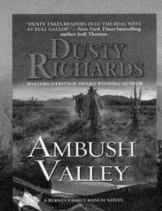

 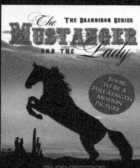 

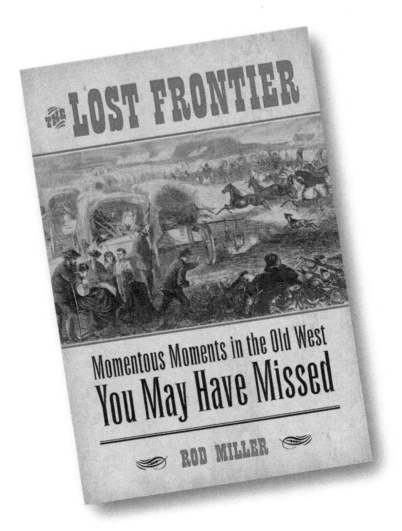

JAILBREAK

A SHORT STORY BY J.B. HOGAN

AUTHOR OF *LOSING COTTON* AND *LIVING BEHIND TIME*

There were seven prisoners in the Ft. Vernon, Missouri county jail. Theo Murray was one of them. He was only seventeen and it didn't seem right to him that he was stuck in that dirty, smelly, dark little jail—imprisoned on a charge of bushwhacking.

Heck, he wasn't no bushwhacker. With his father away fighting the Federals, he'd been left to take care of the family farm and to look out for his mother and his two little sisters. He was plowing behind old Carl the work horse when the riders came up and just plain took him off with them.

One minute he's working in the fields and ten minutes later he's on the back of a horse with a crazy tobacco-chewing outlaw riding hell bent through the Missouri countryside heading for who knew where.

When he looked back to see what had become of his mother and sisters all he could see was a plume of smoke going up from the house. Two riders came up tight alongside the crazy outlaw's horse to make sure Theo couldn't try to escape and run back home.

The leader of the bushwhackers called himself 'major', Major Buck Jacobs—and he was a rough one. He didn't put up with no back talk. The first night Theo was with them, one boy dared to speak up and Jacobs hit him so hard it broke the kid's jaw. The next day they just left that boy in the brush to fend for himself.

For a few days, the gang mostly rode around stealing food and things from farms where the people were out working away from the house. But after Theo had been with them

about a week or two, and was missing his family something fierce, things took a harder turn.

They came up on a well-kept looking place, from the clean yard and barn and all, and the major reined them in just inside a line of trees about an eighth of a mile from the main farm house.

"All right, boys," Jacobs said, "me and Dawson here's going in to parley with these folks. But it's just a dodge. When I take off my hat that's a signal for the rest of you to come riding in with pistols blazing. You got that?"

"Yes, sir," all the boys answered.

They checked their pistols. Nearly every one of them carried four on them at all times. They were loaded, powdered, capped, and ready for firing. Some of the boys could hold one pistol in each hand with the horse reins in their teeth and fire to beat the band. They carried the other two in their belts and swapped them out just as fast as you can imagine. It was a sight to see.

The major and Dawson rode on in and their plan seemed to be working. Jacobs took off his hat and sort of waved it about as if he was making some point or the other. The rest of the outlaws took the cue and went roaring out of the woods cursing and shouting like banshees. The tobacco-chewing outlaw and Theo were left behind holding a handful of spare horses. It was the only job he could trust him with the major had said, and even with that he made sure tobacco boy was nearby with loaded pistols.

Out ahead, the farm people took off in all directions while

Major Jacobs and Dawson fired wildly at them. When the rest of the outlaw band was about halfway to the farm house, all of a sudden out of a stand of trees across the way came a whole pack of blue-clad militia men. They charged the bush-whackers, firing as they rode.

Bullets flew and people dropped. The air filled with smoke. Theo saw at least two of the bushwhackers go down hard off their horses. He saw one horse die. A militia man screamed in agony and fell from his horse, landing flat on his back in front of the farm house. Some exchanges were almost at point blank range. Another bushwhacker fell, a second man in blue followed.

The militia split the bushwhacker charge, drove through the heart of it. Major Jacobs wheeled his horse to the right, towards another part of the woods. He waved his hat and shot once into the air. Even above the din, Theo could hear the major's call for retreat. The bushwhackers reconnoitered with Jacobs and raced away off into the woods, most of the militia men in pursuit.

Three of them broke off and headed for Theo and tobacco boy. Theo ran and hid behind a tree. The tobacco chewer stood his ground, pistols blazing. Suddenly the militia men were upon him, firing down at him. There was a loud splat of one round hitting the boy's head. He staggered backward and fell dead in the woods. The men in blue quickly surrounded Theo, dismounted, and captured him.

"I ain't one of them," he cried, raising his arms in surrender.

"Shut the hell up," a short, stocky militia man said, cuffing him around the head and shoulders. Theo cowered. Another of the soldiers, not so short, not quite so stocky, punched him in the side of the face. He dropped like a felled tree.

"Get up, you damned outlaw," Shorty said.

"I'm gonna shoot him," the third man, an older, bearded fellow, insisted. He aimed his pistol at Theo's head.

Theo cringed.

"I ain't...." he began.

"You ain't worth the powder and ball to kill you," the bearded man said.

The other two laughed. One of them produced a length of rope and they tied Theo's hands behind his back—roughly. They pushed him over and slung him onto one of the extra bushwhacker horses.

"You're lucky we don't string you up out here in the woods," the stocky man snarled.

"The judge'll know what to do with him," the bearded man declared.

• • •

After a couple of days in the dank, dark Ft. Vernon jail, the county judge sentenced Theo to five years for bushwhacking and one year for resisting arrest—both over Theo's feeble, un-legally represented objections.

"You're lucky we don't hang you, boy," the judge said, to the considerable amusement of the militia men who arrested Theo and the two jailers who attended the trial and found it most entertaining to be getting "new meat" for their medieval-looking workplace.

Besides Theo, the prisoners in the Ft. Vernon jail were a mixed bag of local boys gone wrong. Two brothers from over in Nevada were serving time for killing their neighbor over a cow dispute. They hung to themselves in the darkest recesses of the one-celled, low-roofed building.

Three other boys were also in for being bushwhackers and the largest of them, a boy named Zeke, was jail boss—he told everybody else what to do and got the best of the slop they got each day for what was referred to as food. They all claimed to have ridden with Quantrill and the James Boys but Theo didn't know who those people were so he was unimpressed by that knowledge.

The seventh boy, Jeb, was a very nervous kid from out in the county who was serving time for stealing a horse from one of his cousins. The boy claimed to have just borrowed the animal but the cousin insisted it was theft and pressed charges. Jeb and Theo felt terribly wronged by life and so made fast friends in short order.

On the outside, the jail was mostly made of a yellow rock found by the banks of a nearby stream. Inside, it was barely tall enough for a full-sized man to stand. There was a dirt floor and the one cell, which took up most of the space, and only one small, barred window in front. Just inside the door was a cramped area where the jailers sat guard behind a small wooden desk.

The two jailers, one a graying, middle-aged man named Burl and the other, who drank steadily and was called Rummy by the prisoners, alternated twelve-hour shifts babysitting the clientele. Twice a day, a chunky teen-aged girl brought food—usually some kind of gruel-like swill with an unidentifiable hard, dark bread. But it was better than nothing and after Zeke had his pick of it, the other boys worked out a way for everyone to at least get some of the food.

There was a bucket of water on the floor just outside the bars of the cell with a dipper and the boys availed themselves of that as needed. There was a kind of small hole or ditch at a back corner of the cell that they used also as needed and that provided another layer of pungency to the already nearly intolerable atmosphere inside the building.

Every night, Rummy drank himself to sleep well before

midnight and the boys used this time to learn about each other and to work on various schemes that would get them out of the Ft. Vernon jail—the sooner the better. While Zeke held court with Theo, Jeb and his two fellow bushwhackers, Bart and Jace, the cow brothers themselves, stayed to one side participating in their favorite sport—tossing pieces of dirt and bits of rock at the loudly snoring Rummy.

"Boys," Zeke said, "I heard the jailers talking yesterday and they said the Federals is getting antsy because General Stirling Price is forming up an army to chase the Yanks out of Missouri. Me and my boys aim to rejoin Captain Quantrill." He paused to make sure Rummy was still sleeping. "We're busting out of this place as soon as we can figure a way. You can go with us or make it on your own. That's up to each one of you."

"How would we get horses?" Theo asked.

"There's a livery stable just across the way," Zeke answered. "We take 'em out of there."

"But ain't that horse thiefing?" Jeb wondered.

"Good gawd," Zeke hammed it up, "you're in here for horse stealing your ownself and you're worried about taking some to get away from this stinking hell hole?"

"I didn't steal the first one," Jeb mildly objected.

"Right, and I'm the man in the moon and Theo there ain't a bushwhacker either, I suppose?"

"I ain't one neither," Theo said.

"Lord, it is all innocence down in here." Zeke shook his head. "Well, maybe you boys would just as rather stay here when me and my boys bust out then."

"I ain't saying that," Theo countered, then pointed at the cow brothers. "But what about them there?" The brothers stopped throwing bits of the jail floor at Rummy long enough to glance over at Theo and the others.

"Shoot." Zeke laughed. "Them boys don't know nothing about nothing except cows. They won't even know we gone when we go." The cow brothers shrugged their shoulders and went back to their throwing game.

"What if they catch us right away?" Jeb asked. "They'll just add more time onto what we got. They might hang us even."

"Ain't nobody gonna hang us." Zeke snorted. "Hell, we're just kids."

"I seen a guy no older'n you hung down by Sedalia one time," Bart put in.

"Shut up," Zeke told him. "We ain't gonna get caught anyway, much less hung. Now settle down."

"How you think we gonna escape, then, Zeke?" Jace came up beside the cell boss.

"Something will come up. Burl or Rummy will mess up. We'll get out. Maybe that little fat food girl will help us."

"Even if that happens or something," Theo said, "how we get from here to the stable without being seen and then get horses without the stable man seeing us and stopping us?"

"Leave that to me," Zeke said. "I'll take care of it. We need three or four horses, five best, one for each fellow."

"They got that many over there?" Theo wondered.

"Usually more'n that," Zeke said. "The stage stops just up from the livery and swaps out horses. So they usually keep six or eight over there. We won't have no problem with horses. As long as little girl Jeb there don't have no objection to us borrowing a couple to ride out on. Think you can do it, horse thief?"

"I can do it," Jeb answered, "and I ain't no little girl. I'm just as tough as you are."

"Oh, yeah, you little…"

Zeke moved towards Jeb but Theo stepped between them. Bart and Jace surrounded Theo. The boys eyed each other, waiting for somebody to make a move. Then Zeke laughed and backed away from Theo.

"Easy boys," Zeke smiled. "No reason for us to fight each other. It's Rummy over there and Burl that's our enemy not our ownselves." The other boys eased back. "But when we bust out, maybe it's better we go our separate ways."

"Sounds about right," Theo agreed.

"We're gonna go north and meet back up with Quantrill, right Zeke?" Jace asked.

"That's exactly what we're gonna do. How about you two?" Zeke pointed at Theo and Jeb.

"I'm heading south," Theo said. "I want to find Prices's army and come back up here and chase these Yankees off our land. We're defending our homes," he added, "from the… from the… northern aggression. Yeah, that's what Major Jacobs always called it. The War of Northern Aggression. Yes, sir."

"Well, that's real patriotic of you," Zeke said with a smirk. "Me and the boys follow Captain Quantrill. We defend our homes, too, but we do it freer. No army rules. We do as we please, take what we want, live off the land, live off what we get. Some people might call it stealing but the captain calls it appropriating for the cause." Zeke and his two pals guffawed at that.

"Each to his own," Theo walked away from Zeke towards the end of the cell farthest from the smelly pit in the back. "Live and let live, that's what my pa always said."

"That's damn straight." Zeke sniffed, turning to watch Rummy as the jailer stirred long enough to take a last drink from his cup. Zeke picked up some dirt off the cell floor and like the cow brothers tossed it at Rummy, who didn't seem to notice as he immediately laid his head back down on his arms and went back to snoring. "That is definitely damn straight."

• • •

Around noon on a warm, sunny day, Burl the jailer took the cow brothers out of the cell. The circuit judge had come to town unannounced and told the law men he had something he wanted to talk to the brothers about. That left the other prisoners alone in the dingy calaboose. For a while, they banged around on the cell bars, hoping to find a weak spot but to no avail. After a few more half-hearted attempts they gave up the effort and went back to their usual state of inactivity and boredom.

It was later in the afternoon when the cow brothers were returned to jail and Rummy brought them back. He was already three sheets to the wind and half-staggered as he pushed his prisoners into the cell. Just as Rummy was about to lock the cell, the little food girl came in.

"Come on in here, sweetheart," he slurred, stumbling back from the cell. "What you got there?"

"Food for the prisoners, sir," the girl said shyly.

"Kind of early ain't you?" Rummy leered.

"I don't know sir." the girl timidly approached the cell.

Rummy shuffled over, devouring her with his bloodshot eyes. She leaned away from him but he put his arms around her shoulders, allowing one hand to drape over her and lightly touch a breast. The girl squealed, threw the prisoners' food down by the cell, and fought herself free from Rummy.

"Don't be that way," he mumbled, as the girl hurried for the jail door. "Well, hell," he cursed after she had escaped. "I just wanted to have some fun."

Producing a bottle from somewhere, Rummy went to the jail desk, picked up his usual drinking cup, and filled it with liquor. He sat down with a loud grunt and made fast work of emptying the cup.

Over in the cell, Bart realized what had happened. He came up to the door and stood by it.

"Shhh," Zeke, who also had seen, put a finger to his mouth. He looked over at the cow brothers. They backed away towards the far side of the cell.

Zeke and the others watched Rummy then. Watched him keep drinking. Watched as he got progressively sleepier, finally passing out with his head on his arms on top of the desk. The prisoners kept watching.

"Zeke," Jace said, "see…."

"Hush," Zeke said. "Quiet. Wait."

Theo and Jeb joined Zeke and his boys by the cell door.

"Give it just a spell more," Zeke said.

When Rummy began snoring loudly, Zeke tried the cell door. It opened out easily. They were steps from freedom.

"You goin'?" Zeke asked the cow brothers, who remained in the shadows.

"No," one of them answered. "Judge says they's a good chance we getting out soon."

"On appeal," the other one added. "We cain't take the chance on the running."

"Suit yourself," Zeke said, and he and the others hustled out of the cell.

Bart lifted Rummy's gun right from its holster and handed it to Zeke. Jace took a rifle out of a case behind the desk. Theo found another pistol in a drawer. Zeke and he exchanged looks.

GORDON
bonnet
www.gordonbonnet.com
twitter.com@TalesOfWhoa

"We need protection, too," Theo said.

"Okay," Zeke said. "Now listen boys, we peek out and see what's up, then hustle over to that livery stable and get the hell out of here. Act regular when you come out so's no one thinks anything of us."

The boys' luck held again. The streets were deserted, everyone apparently already home for supper. They walked quickly over to the livery stable. There were plenty of horses in there and the stable man was in the back pitching some hay. Zeke signaled for Bart and Jace to go in the front and go up to the man. He, Theo, and Jeb hurried around to a side door.

"Hey, what are you boys doing in here?" the stable man asked when he saw Bart and Jace moving towards him. He walked up to them. "Who are you?"

"Well, sir…." Bart began. He was cut off by Zeke coming up behind the man and knocking him stone cold with the barrel of Rummy's pistol. The man hit the ground with a low groan.

With a speed no doubt engendered by the imminence of freedom, the boys rapidly saddled a horse each and were ready to ride. Zeke held them up at the front of the livery.

"Like I said before, you can go with us, if you want," he told Theo and Jeb, who were mounted to his left. "We're heading north, to find Captain Quantrill. He always needs men."

"Thanks anyway," Theo replied. "I reckon we'll still head south. We plan to join up with General Price and drive these here aggressors from our land."

"Suit yourself," Zeke said. Then to Bart and Jace, "Ready boys?"

"Ready," they confirmed.

"So long fellows," Zeke called, he and his boys spurred their mounts and shot out of the livery onto the town road with a whoop of joy. They headed right, to the north.

Theo and Jeb rode to the left, south, keeping their horses at an easy trot at first. In a moment, though, they could hear the town begin to stir. Then some shouts. The report of a rifle, scattered pistol fire.

The boys pushed their horses to a gallop then, fleeing the town with all the speed the animals could muster, hellbent for southern Missouri. If General Price was forming up a unit to make a big run at the Yankees, it was time to be a part of it.

Being in the regular army couldn't be no worse than having been arrested for being a bushwhacker or a horse thief or locked up as a prisoner in the Ft. Vernon jail. It seemed like the best thing to do right this minute and so they rode hard, hard away from Ft. Vernon, hard towards the south and General Price. Dust billowed up behind them as they rode. They never looked back.

J.B. Hogan

J. B. Hogan is a prolific and award-winning author. He grew up in Fayetteville, Arkansas, but moved to Southern California in 1961 before entering the United States Air Force in 1964. Among many other adventures at home and abroad during his years in the service, he served under famed Air Force General Chuck Yeager in Korea. After the military, though, he went back to college, receiving a Ph.D. in English from Arizona State University in 1979.

J. B. has published over 250 stories and poems and six books, including the novels *The Apostate, Living Behind Time* and *Losing Cotton*, a book of poetry and short fiction titled *The Rubicon, Fallen,* a collection of short stories, and a local baseball history book, *Angels in the Ozarks*. Each of them are available on Amazon.com. His newest book, the 1930's noir mystery *Tin Hollow*, will be published in August from Shannon Press.

J.B. also serves as Past President of the Washington County (AR) Historical Society. He plays upright bass in East of Zion, a family band that specializes in bluegrass-flavored Americana music.

Find out more about J.B. at www.thejbhogan.com.

indian TERRITORY

John T. Biggs
native american columnist

"If you can't beat them, join them," was the motto of the Five Civilized Tribes who dominated the southeastern United States in the late 18th and early 19th centuries. For almost two hundred years the Spanish, the French, and the English sent explorers, soldiers, and colonists to the new world. Then American colonists established a European-style government complete with a political system and a well-armed military. It was clear these inconvenient immigrants from the wrong side of the Atlantic weren't going away.

It seemed so innocent in the beginning. The wooden ships and the pale-skinned men who sailed them were exotic curiosities. The Europeans were friendly, generous with trade goods, and there weren't many of them—certainly not enough to cause real trouble for the millions of Indians with roots in the New World that reached back thousands of years. So they welcomed the white explorers. They shared food, drank from the same cups, passed around ceremonial pipes, treated them like visiting dignitaries who were surely just passing through.

It seemed like witchcraft when people started getting sick. Within weeks of the first contact smallpox, typhus, measles, influenza, and diphtheria spread across the land in all directions. In a matter of a few decades ninety percent of Indians on the eastern coast of North America were dead.

While the tribes were in chaos, white emigrants established

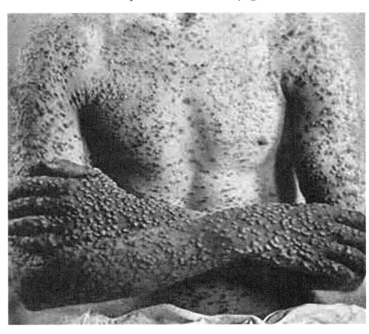

Smallpox swept the east coast of North America within decades of the arrival of the first Europeans.

By the time of the Indian Removal Act of 1830, the civilized tribes had adopted European style housing, and farming methods.

permanent settlements. They brought agriculture, metal tools, guns, a new religion, and something called land ownership—a totally foreign concept to the Indians.

The Cherokee and the four Muskogee speaking tribes (Choctaw, Chickasaw, Creek, and Seminole) saw the futility of resisting the legions of newcomers and decided to get on board. They learned English. They adopted European clothing styles and religions. Their houses and farms were indistinguishable from the white emigrants'.

The Indians ceded tribal land rather than come into conflict with the new government. They sent their children to white missionary schools and—except for the Seminole—even started buying black slaves. The Five Civilized Tribes did everything they could to fit in to the new world order and it looked like they might actually stand a chance of making it.

The U.S. government, starting with President George Washington, followed a policy of acculturation they hoped would shift tribal territories into the hands of white citizens with little or no military action. Thomas Jefferson summed it up: "We shall push our trading uses, and be glad to see the good and influential individuals among them run in debt, because we observe that when these debts get beyond what the individuals can pay, they become willing to lop them off by a cession of lands." The Indians would fall into the credit trap that had been sending Europeans into debtors' prisons and indentured servitude for centuries.

Things didn't go the way the politicians planned. The civilized tribes put modern agricultural practices to work and flourished. Their children learned to read and write. They intermarried with white citizens and learned the ins and outs of politics and commerce. They sold surplus crops locally, cultivated more land, and planted highly marketable crops like tobacco and cotton. When the cotton gin came into widespread use the tribes turned their communal farms into a profitable international businesses.

Andrew Jackson

By the time Andrew Jackson was elected president in 1829, white Americans in the southeast were hungry for the agricultural land owned by the five tribes. They were envious of the Indians' success and suspicious of their relationships with foreign governments who still had substantial interests in the New World. White plantation farmers were especially suspicious of the Seminoles, who welcomed runaway slaves into their tribe. Tensions between the white government and the Indians came to a head when the Seminoles and about half of the Creek sided with the British in the War of 1812.

President Jackson considered the elimination of the Indians inevitable. "Humanity has often wept over the fate of the aborigines of this country and philanthropy has long been busily employed in devising means to avert it, but its progress has never for a moment been arrested, and one by one have many powerful tribes disappeared from the earth."

Previous presidents had negotiated with the Five Tribes as

Andrew Jackson, the general who won the Creek War, the Seminole War, and was instrumental in winning the War of 1812, was elected President in 1829. He quickly pushed the Indian Removal Act of 1830 through Congress.

Four of the Civilized Tribes (the Seminoles excluded) owned African slaves.

separate independent nations. Jackson decided to solve the "Indian problem" with a single piece of legislation backed up with a well-armed military. He signed the Indian Removal Act into law in 1830. Except for very small reservations, all the land of the Five Tribes east of the Mississippi River would be ceded to the government in exchange for assigned lands in the newly created Indian Territory on the unsettled side of the Mississippi.

The Treaty of Dancing Rabbit Creek

No tribe worked harder than the Choctaw to fit into the dominant white U.S. culture. They did not stage armed insurrections, didn't make treaties with foreign governments, had no firebrand leaders bent on returning to the old ways; the tribe had actually assisted General Andrew Jackson in the Creek Wars fifteen years before the passage of the Indian Removal Act and peacefully ceded thousands of acres of their homeland. Since they were the most cooperative of the tribes, President Jackson decided they would be the first to go.

He summoned three Principal Chiefs (Greenwood LeFlore, Musholatubbee, and Nittucachee) and a number of lesser Choctaw leaders to a meeting in Franklin, Tennessee where they could be persuaded to sign a removal treaty. The Chiefs opposed holding a meeting where there would be no Choctaw witnesses, but they agreed to meet with government representatives at a site in the southwestern corner of Choctaw land in a place known as Dancing Rabbit Creek. There, the U.S. government made the Indians an offer they could not refuse. Two hundred chiefs and headmen signed a treaty agreeing to trade their eleven million acre homeland in what is now the state of Mississippi for fifteen million acres in the newly created Indian Territory—what would ultimately be the state of Oklahoma.

The Choctaw believed the move would be gradual and voluntary, but it started less than a year after the Treaty of Dancing Rabbit Creek was signed. The details of the forced removal were handled by private contractors but the military stood by in case the Indians required persuasion.

Chief George Harkins (nephew of Chief Greenwood LeFlore) wrote an open letter to America when the first stage in the three-stage removal began in the fall of 1831. Among other things, he said, "We as Choctaws rather chose to suffer and be free, than live under the degrading influence of laws, which our voice could not be heard in their formation ... Much as the state of Mississippi has wronged us, I cannot find in my heart any other sentiment than an ardent wish for her prosperity and happiness."

By the end of 1833, all but a few thousand Choctaw had been moved to Indian Territory. Some of them were crowded onto barges and towed down the Mississippi River and back up the Arkansas River. Most of them were force-marched across Arkansas Territory during record cold winters. Four thousand Choctaw died of disease during the removal—mostly of cholera.

Things didn't go well for the few Choctaw who stayed behind. In 1849, members of the Mississippi Band described their situation: "We have had our habitations torn down and burned, our fences destroyed, cattle turned into our fields and we ourselves have been scourged, manacled, fettered and otherwise personally abused, until by such treatment some of our best men have died."

Remaining families continued moving out of Mississippi to join the Choctaw Nation in Oklahoma until well into the early 20th century.

At Dancing Rabbit Creek, 200 chiefs and lesser headmen signed a treaty that would trade their 11 million acre homeland in what is now Mississippi for 15 million acres in the newly created Indian Territory.

Greenwood LeFlore (principal Chief of the Choctaw at the time of the removal) did not travel to Indian Territory with his people. He was given an allotment of land and remained in Mississippi.

Chief Greenwood LeFlore's plantation home in what became the state of *Mississippi.*

The Muskogee Creek

Right after The Great Comet of 1811 a Shawnee mystic named Tecumseh visited the Creek Confederacy. He preached against war and torture, but also against cooperation with the U.S. government. Tecumseh was dead set against further cession of tribal lands and believed that it could be stopped if the tribes (especially the southeastern tribes) united. He promised the Great Spirit would send a sign of support for his ideas shortly after he left. A few months later, the New Madrid Earthquake shook Muskogee lands. As with every sign from the Great Spirit there were differences in interpretation.

Tecumseh's visit and the tremor that followed triggered a civil war among the Creek. Most of the tribe elected to cooperate with the U.S. Government and hope for the best, but a sizable minority united with the Tecumseh Federation and actively resisted white efforts to occupy tribal land. Since this happened just as the War of 1812 was breaking out, it put a faction of the tribe on the side of the British in direct conflict with General Andrew Jackson.

On August 9, 1814, the general forced the Creek to sign the Treaty of Fort Jackson, requiring them to cede 23 million acres—half of Alabama and part of southern Georgia—to the United States government. He made no concessions to the Creek who had not supported the Tecumseh Federation.

Eight years later, President Andrew Jackson forced the Creek to sign the Treaty of Cusseta, relinquishing their remaining lands east of the Mississippi and accepting "voluntary" removal to Indian Territory. The Army force-marched nearly 20,000 Creek across Tennessee and Arkansas starting in 1834. Three thousand five hundred Indians died in the process.

President Jackson promised the Muskogee Creek this about their new homeland inside Indian Territory: "There your white brothers will not trouble you; they will have no claim to the land, and you can live upon it you and all your children, as long as the grass grows or the water runs, in peace and plenty. It will be yours forever."

It seemed that any time the U.S. government tied ownership of land to water and grass trouble was sure to follow.

The Cherokee

The Georgia militia had been harassing the Cherokee since the Compact of 1802, in which President Thomas Jefferson promised to extinguish all Indian titles to land in the state. The harassment accelerated after gold was discovered on tribal land in 1828. The militia kidnapped Principal Chief John Ross in 1835 and tried to intimidate the 18,000 Cherokee into accepting Andrew Jackson's removal policy. The kidnapping failed but it opened the door to another treacherous tactic.

When Ross was released he traveled to Washington D.C. and tried to negotiate more reasonable terms with Andrew Jackson for the removal of his tribe. He lobbied Congress unsuccessfully to exclude the Cherokee from the removal policy. He sued the state of Georgia in the U.S. Supreme Court and won an unenforceable ruling that prevented the militia from imposing the Compact of 1802.

The Cherokee were subject to laws and regulations in which they had no voice, but John Ross was intent on resisting the removal policy as loudly and as publicly as possible. The high death rate during the removal of the Choctaw and the Creek, and the continuing fierce resistance of the Seminole added weight to his arguments, especially in the more liberal northern states that didn't stand to profit from the seizure of Cherokee land.

While Chief John Ross was in Washington, President Jackson's agents assembled a small group of dissident Cherokee in the tribal capital of New Echota, Georgia, and

This is a representation of what the Great Comet of 1811 must have looked like. It was the largest and brightest comet in recorded history, and remained so until the Hale-Bopp Comet in 1997.

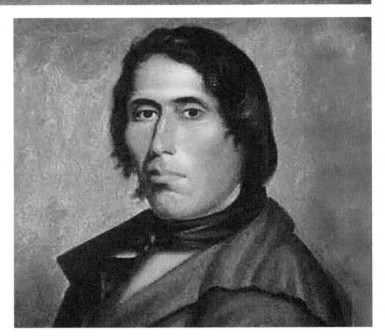

Tecumseh, the Shawnee prophet who convinced the Creek and their Seminole allies to resist the U.S. government.

persuaded them to sign the Treaty of New Echota, giving the president and the state of Georgia everything they wanted.

The Cherokee tribes collected a list of 13,000 signatures of tribal members opposed to this unauthorized treaty and presented it to Congress. In spite of the protests, the treaty was ratified in the U.S. Senate by a single vote and signed into law by President Andrew Jackson.

Removal took place in three stages:

Voluntary Removal—Members of the tribe who were in favor of the treaty were assisted by the government.

Forced Removal—Members of the tribe opposed to the treaty were placed in internment camps during the hottest part of the summer of 1838.

Reluctant Removal—After being held in the internment camps, the reluctant Cherokee were forced to travel across country to their new home in Indian Territory. Two thousand Cherokee died in the internment camps and another two thousand perished on the forced march across the country.

The Seminole

The Seminole didn't start out as a tribe. They were a mix of breakaway Muskogee, and runaway African slaves who took refuge in the swampy lands of southern Georgia and central Florida in territory claimed by the Spanish, the English, and the Americans, but actually wanted by no one. Their name might be a corruption of cimarron, the Spanish word for wild, or it might be derived from the Muskogee term *yat'siminoli*, which means free people.

The United States probably wouldn't have gone to so much trouble to remove them if they hadn't been so zealous in their opposition to slavery and refusal to obey the laws of the white government. Along with a breakaway faction of the Creek, the Seminole took the side of the British in the war of 1812, primarily because Britain had no plans to bring them under her control.

The United States spent an estimated $20,000,000 to defeat the Seminole in the second Seminole War, more than the removal costs of all the other tribes combined. Although the U.S. did sign the Treaty of Payne's Landing with the Seminole, the tribe never went peacefully to their assigned lands in Indian Territory. They were captured in small numbers beginning in 1832 and continuing through the 1840s and transported in shackles along with runaway slaves (Black Seminoles) who had joined the tribe.

The Chickasaw

With all the bad press the United States had received in removing the Choctaw, Creek, Cherokee, and Seminole, the Chickasaw were in an excellent position to negotiate. Rather than trade their homeland in what is now Mississippi, Alabama, Kentucky, and Tennessee for assigned land in Indian Territory, the Chickasaw sold their land to the U.S. for $3,000,000 and purchased territory from the Choctaw Nation for $530,000.

They were a relatively small tribe—roughly 5,000 including approximately 1,200 black slaves. They traveled along the same general route as the Choctaw from 1837 through 1847. About eight hundred Chickasaw died during the removal.

—John T. Biggs is a critically-acclaimed writer with four novels and over sixty published short stories to his credit. When not travelling the globe with his wife, he makes his home in Oklahoma City, Oklahoma.

Principal Chief John Ross. While he was in Washington lobbying for relief from the Indian Removal act, Government agents persuaded lesser chiefs and headmen to sign the Treaty of New Eschota, giving Georgia and the U.S. Government everything they wanted.

Osceola led the Seminole war of resistance when the U.S. government tried to remove the Seminole from their lands in southern Georgia and Florida. He was captured in 1837 under a deceptive flag of truce. He died a few months later in prison.

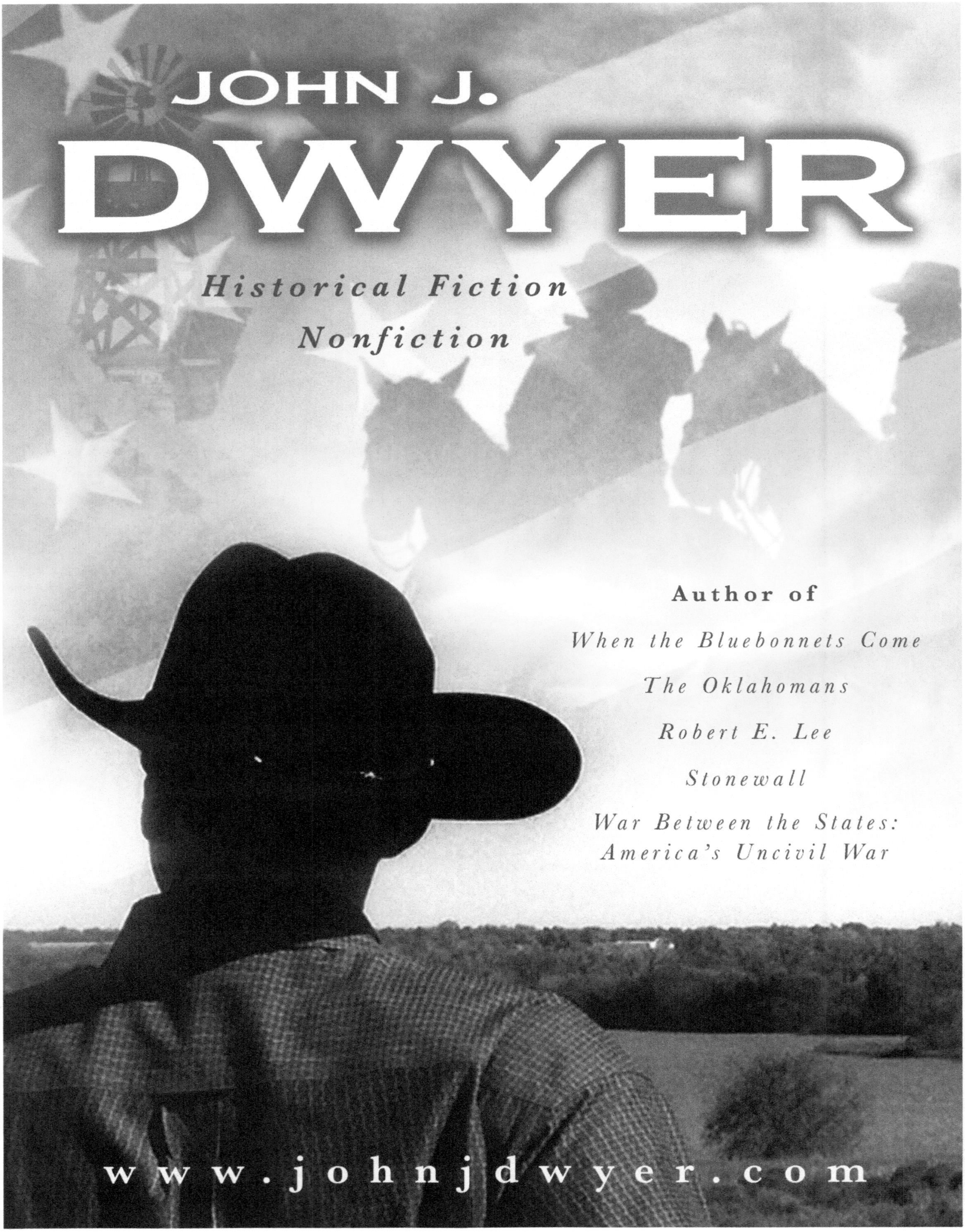

JOHN J. DWYER

Historical Fiction

Nonfiction

Author of

When the Bluebonnets Come

The Oklahomans

Robert E. Lee

Stonewall

War Between the States: America's Uncivil War

www.johnjdwyer.com

A SHORT STORY

I KNOW WHAT YOU ARE

Dan Robichaux stood on a hill at sunset looking down on the dusty streets of Safford, Arizona. The heat rising from the rocks beneath his boot soles was at least more bearable than it'd been when he walked out into the desert at a little after noon. He'd promised Josh Bailey help building a fence that afternoon, but that was too bad.

The itchy feeling in the pit of his belly had come back. He knew what that meant all too well.

There was no use walking off into the searing heat, looking for a rocky arroyo in which to hide. Didn't matter where he went, she'd find him. It might take a day or two, but it'd happen.

He knew this from his days working on a fishing boat out of Delcambre, Louisiana, when he'd been Anatole instead of Dan, when there was nothing to eat but what they caught. His father and two older brothers were dead, two at Shiloh and one at Antietam, and if it hadn't been for his share of the fish and what they could grow in their scrawny plot of vegetables, he and his mother and sister would have starved to death.

Didn't stop you from cutting and running when she showed up.

He was disgusted at himself for his cowardice. Shortly after his sixteenth birthday was the first time he saw her, when he was barely a man, only just needing to shave, but interested enough in women to go to the fais-do-do in the evening instead of collapsing into bed. That was when she appeared, dressed in white, a knowing smile on her face. Did she want to dance? From her expression, it looked like she might be interested in more than that.

He went up to her, wearing an eager grin, heat rising in his face and groin simultaneously. Then her smile became a leer, her delicate features twisting into a snarl.

"Anatole Robichaux," she said. "I know what you are."

And she turned and vanished into the gloom.

No one else saw her that night, no one heard what she said. But two days later, the fisherman he worked for, Calixte Larivière, came up to him with a grin. "*Qui est-ce, cette fille en blanc?*" and elbowed Dan in the ribs.

"*Quelle fille?*" Dan asked.

"The fancy girl in the white dress hangin' around the pier askin' for you. Prospère and Antoine said she was pretty. She said she wanted you." Another elbow in the ribs.

In the days that followed, person after person asked him about the beautiful girl in white, porcelain skin, copper hair, who had only one interest. "Where is Anatole Robichaux? When you see him, tell him I know him."

It was only when she started telling people what she knew about him that he fled west from Delcambre. First to Houston, where he learned cattle and horses and worked eight months as a ranch hand before she found him and he had to run again. Next in San Antonio, then Fort Stockton, and Las Cruces, and each time after a few months' respite, she'd be there.

I know what you are, Anatole Robichaux.

He'd hoped Safford would be far enough away. But apparently not. The itch right behind his navel was back. It always meant she was near.

He could keep going. California wasn't far, even if high

around the campfire

summer was one of the worst times to try to get there. But then where? You run into the Pacific Ocean, you stop there. Trapped. At that point, he'd have to face her, like a jackrabbit cornered by a coyote.

The dry wind brushed his face, bringing him back to the present. She'd found him. God knew how, but she'd found him again.

There was no choice but to face her. He couldn't leave that night, much as he wanted to. A trip farther west would take provisioning—if he got on his horse and headed out into the desert at this time of year, he'd die.

So he steeled his gut against his fear, and started to walk back into Safford and… her.

But damned if he wouldn't have a drink first. Jeb Mitchell, barkeep and owner of the Silver Star Saloon, would at least have a joke or a story to lift his spirits. That, and whiskey aplenty.

And sure enough, Mitchell's creased face lit up with a grin as Dan walked in.

"Dan, you rascal," he said in a growl.

Faces turned, most welcoming, others grim and suspicious. Had she already talked to people? No way to tell but to wait and see what happened.

"Bailey's hotter'n hell," Mitchell said. "Said you left him workin' by hisself. He's a man you don't wanna tick off, son, thought you knew that."

Dan shrugged. "Had no choice."

"Tell him that."

"I will. Double whiskey."

Mitchell looked at him with an eyebrow raised, but poured the drink. "Where you been all day?"

"None o' your damn business."

"Maybe not, but Bailey's gonna make it his business, seein' as how he's payin' your wages. Better have a better story come up with than 'none o' your damn business.'"

Dan scowled down into his whiskey, took a big swallow, and grimaced.

Mort Cavanaugh, another of Bailey's hired help, gave a snort of a laugh, and said across the room, "He's got a woman on his mind, Mitchell. Pretty one, too."

Dan closed his eyes, and didn't turn toward the mocking voice. It was all playing out again, just as it had in Las Cruces, Fort Stockton, San Antonio….

"That it, boy?" Mitchell chuckled. "You chasin' some pretty skirt when you should be workin' for Mr. Bailey?"

Dan tried to answer, but the negatives wouldn't come together in his brain. Defending himself again? And from what?

And who?

But Cavanaugh wasn't done. "Sweet little thing. Hair like polished copper and skin like cream. Voice is gentle like music. And she come up to me, me and Luke Ivins, and says, 'I'm looking for Anatole Robichaux. Maybe you know him as Dan. When you see him, tell him I want him.'"

The bartender gave a low whistle. "Sakes, boy, I didn't know you was keepin' a woman on the side…."

Dan tossed back the rest of the whiskey in one gulp and slammed the glass on the bar. He glared first Mitchell, then Cavanaugh, into silence.

Go ahead. I dare you to say one more damn word.

They didn't. He had a reputation as a man who wasn't afraid to use his fists if provoked. Cavanaugh looked scared—he always was a blusterer on the surface and yellow at the core. Mitchell just looked surprised.

He turned and pushed his way out into the street, punching the door so hard he nearly took it off the hinges.

Back to the bunkhouse where he and Josh Bailey's other workers slept. She'd find him sooner or later no matter what he did. May as well let it happen. After that, though… then what?

• • •

It turned out to be sooner.

Dan had undressed in the dark, climbed into his bed, and pulled up a rough blanket to mid-chest when the itching just behind his navel suddenly grew worse. He winced, opened his eyes, and looked around. The room was completely dark. The only sounds were the snores of his bunkmates, Tom and Ben MacLennan, only arrived last month from Scotland. They were sound sleepers—they wouldn't awaken unless somebody kicked the wall down.

"Anatole," came a light, gentle voice, all too familiar.

"What?" His voice came out in snarled whisper.

"I know what you are."

He sat up, the blanket slipping from his bare chest into his lap. "Where are you?"

"Outside."

He stood up, clad only in his underwear, and went to the door and threw it open. And there she was, just like in Las Cruces, Fort Stockton… all the way back to the first time he'd seen her, at the fais-do-do in Delcambre. Slender, with smooth cream skin, long coppery hair gleaming in the moonlight, clad in a white dress that clung to her curves in a way that should have been enticing but now, after all these years, was repellant.

"What do you want with me?"

She gave a clear, gentle laugh. "It's not what I want with you, Anatole. It's what you want with me, remember?"

Dan clenched his fists so hard that his nails dug into his palms. "Why are you following me? Why can't you leave me be?"

She smiled, showing a row of perfect white teeth. "But you know that, too, don't you? I won't leave you be because I know what you are."

"Oh? And what am I?"

"A murderer."

Every time he heard it—what, eight times now? Ten?

More?—it felt like a knife in the gut. He tried to stop himself from responding, knowing what her answer would be, but the words came out through clenched teeth.

"I never killed no one."

"Except for me." The smile became a sardonic sneer. "Do I need to tell you a hundred times?"

"But I never killed you!" His voice rose to a shout. "I never killed no one! I never even laid a finger on you!"

"Oh, my dear," she said. "But you know why you won't admit it, of course." She leaned forward and put her mouth next to his ear. He could feel her cool breath on his face. "That's because it hasn't happened yet."

Then she turned and walked off, hips swaying alluringly, and disappeared into the night.

There was a noise behind him, and standing in the doorway, wearing nothing but a sleepy scowl, was Ben MacLennan.

"Danny," he said, "what in the hell are you yellin' at, this time o' night? Woke me up out of a fine dream, you did."

"Go back to bed, Ben," Dan said in a growl. "It's nothing concernin' you."

Ben snorted. "All right, then. But keep your brawlin' to the daylight hours if you want to keep your friends, lad."

• • •

Over the next three days, Dan saw the girl in the white dress three more times. People came up to him and asked him who the pretty lady was who kept asking about town for him. On the third day, though, things began to turn, as they always did. He got sidewise glances as he went into the Silver Star. Jeb Mitchell got him his drink without a smile, without a joke, smacked it down on the bar in front of him and backed off with a suspicious glare.

Dan didn't have to ask what was wrong. He knew. The girl had done it again. Started a whispering campaign of gossip against him, hinted that he was a killer, that he had strangled an innocent girl and was likely to do it again. That he was on the run, wanted for a hanging offense. Trying to keep one step ahead of the law, a quick trial, and his neck in a noose.

It only remained to see how long it would take before it became intolerable, before he'd have to leave Safford. Exactly as he'd left the other towns. Exactly as he'd probably leave the next town he went to, and the next, until he ran out of places to run.

Dan hunched morosely over his double whiskey at the Silver Star, ignored by the bartender, getting nothing but skew glances from the regulars. Only Ben MacLennan came up to him, a broad grin on his face. Ben was apparently one of the few people in town who hadn't yet seen the girl in the white dress, and he was not the type who gave much heed to gossip.

"Looks like Safford's goin' back on the high road," Ben said, taking a swig of his own drink.

"Whaddya mean?" Dan tried to keep the surly anger from his voice, with little success. Didn't matter. Even though Ben was still friendly, it wouldn't last. It never did.

"Methodist parson rode into town this afternoon. Scowlin' gentleman. Already talkin' 'bout demon rum and closin' down the Silver Star. Ain't heard yet how he plans to do it, bein' as he'll be workin' single-handed."

"Preachers are never content unless they're meddlin' in everyone's business," Dan said.

"Truth, laddie. But at least he brought a fine-lookin' daughter with him. Don't know how a broodin' old goat like him ever found a woman who'd share his bed, but musta happened at least once. She's a fair lass, she is, the likes o' which I ain't seen since I left Stirling. Red hair, hair like shinin' copper…"

The bartender shot Ben a curious and not very friendly glance.

"… dressed all in white, clingin' about her so's you could make a good guess 'bout what was underneath…"

Dan stood so suddenly Ben flinched back, his hand jerking, splashing some of his drink on the bar. Dan's eyes were frozen, his gaze focused on a point far distant.

"What's ailin' you, lad? You can't tell me you're not glad we've got a new lady in town?"

Dan didn't answer, but made his way to the door. He felt as if he'd gone blind. He struck his hip against a table, heard an angry voice shout, "Watch where you're going, you murderin' snake," but barely registered it.

Outside, the sun was setting over the hills, painting the sky with streaks of crimson, scarlet, and gold. He stumbled down the middle of the street toward the bunkhouse.

Would he find out, finally, who his tormentor was? She had never revealed her name. He'd asked, more than once, always received an answer of, "You'll know one day." Now she was traveling with her Methodist minister father. He'd confront her, perhaps the father as well, find out why she had followed him for years. Put an end to it.

He stopped, leaning for support against a post supporting the awning over Lem's Barber Shop. What if she wasn't the same girl? There were other copper-haired lasses in the world. And Ben MacLennan had said she and her father had just arrived that day, but Dan and others had seen the girl in white many times in town over the past three.

Had to be a coincidence. Here he was about to bluster in and demand to see the parson's daughter, making a damn fool of himself and accomplishing nothing.

A harsh voice spoke behind him. "I'm closed."

He turned his head. Lem Mayhew, the barber, stood in his doorway, his face tight, closed, unfriendly.

"I'm not here to get my hair cut."

"Don't matter. I'm closed. Move along."

"You know where that Methodist minister is stayin'? One who just got here today?"

The question appeared to take Lem by surprise.

Maybe he'll think I'm turnin' to God. Givin' up my murderin' ways.

"Hear tell he was stayin' up at Fahey's Inn, till he can build hisself somethin'." Lem's brows drew together again. "Good idea you go talk to him," he said in a sneering voice. "Maybe he'll have some advice for you."

Yeah. Advice. Maybe advice and something else besides.

He turned away, heard Lem slam the door behind him.

Fahey's was the only respectable inn in Safford, and even that was a stretch. At least it was a cut above the rooms over the Silver Star, the only other place for travelers to stay in town, which had seen action as a whorehouse before Jeb Mitchell cleared the place out and raised its reputation a notch. Mike Fahey, the owner, at least kept his place clean. It certainly was the only option in town for an upstanding minister and his daughter.

If she is his daughter.

He once again had to stop himself.

Hang on. You don't know it's her.

But he knew in his heart that it was.

So one way or the other, this'll end tonight. I'm not leaving without answers.

As soon as he walked in and caught Mike Fahey's eye, he knew that the innkeeper heard the whispering about Dan's past. He recognized the expression, how their manners changed, how they treated you different because of it.

My past. My past that hasn't happened yet.

But Fahey's eyes narrowed, and his body stiffened. "Whaddya want here?" His voice held a threat like thunderclouds.

"I'm lookin' for the minister feller, just arrived today."

"Whaddya want with him?"

"I ain't gonna kill him, 'cause I know that's what you're thinkin', Mike Fahey. You been listenin' to rumors, and if you'll listen to me instead I'll tell you they're lies. But I ain't standin' here discussin' that right now. I want to see the minister."

Fahey's face showed doubt. "I won't be havin' blood spilled in my inn."

"Won't be none. Just tell me where he is."

"Upstairs. Second on the left."

Dan nodded, walked past the innkeeper, then up the creaking stairs to the second floor.

Knocked. Heart pounding. Sweat staining his shirt.

The door opened to reveal a dark, ill-favored man with a neat goatee. He regarded Dan with a critical eye, and said, "Yes?"

"I'm looking for the minister."

"I'm Reverend Collins."

"You just got here today?"

"This afternoon, yes."

"Brought your daughter with you?"

Reverend Collins looked fierce. "Why is that your concern?"

"I need to talk to her."

"You'll do no such thing. I won't tolerate such impertinence."

"I don't care what you'll tolerate. I need to talk to her."

A sweet, familiar voice spoke behind him. "Who is it, father? What does he want?"

Dan peered around the scowling minister, and there, dressed in white, her coppery hair gleaming in the lantern light, was…

… her. But when her eyes met his, and there was nothing, no gleam of recognition, no knowing little smile. She raised an eyebrow and said, "Who are you and what do you want with me?"

"You…" Dan choked out. "I know you! I know what you are!"

"What?" she said, her fair skin blanching. "What are you saying? I've never seen you before."

"Never you mind that, Sara. I'll handle this." He drew himself up, although even then he was a good six inches shorter than Dan. "You'll go the way you came, young man. And don't come near my daughter. I know all about roughs like you. Don't think you can bluster your way in here. I'm a man of God, but I have a gun and know how to use it to protect me and mine."

For a moment, Dan considered shoving his way past the minister, demanding that the girl tell him what he wanted to know. But there had been something in her face, that face that was the same as it had been in dozens of encounters, that was still fundamentally different. There was no hint of the certainty, the wicked knowingness, that he'd seen in her before. It didn't take any figuring to see that she had no idea who he was.

Defeated, he turned and went down the stairs, past Mike Fahey's curious and hostile eyes, and out into the night.

How many days left, before the townspeople got the sheriff involved, and Dan was once again forced to leave? And where would he go? He was tired, falling-down tired. Maybe it would be easier to let the sheriff arrest him, jail him, maybe even hang him for killing, years before he met her, a girl who was still alive. He laughed, a tight, harsh laugh that tore him as it escaped. This was absurd. Why wouldn't anyone believe him? Why....

"Anatole Robichaux."

He looked up, and there she was again, dressed in white, eyes glittering and accusatory in the moonlight. But now she wore the familiar expression of hatred and disdain.

"What do you want from me?" he shouted. "Who are you?"

"I'm Sara Collins, don't you remember?"

"I just met you. You say you're a ghost, that I murdered you years ago."

"I never said that. I told you plainly that you will murder me. And you will, unless I can stop you."

"Why would I murder you? I don't know you."

"Because it is what you were born to do. From the moment I saw you back at the dance in Louisiana, I knew it. Murderer." She spat out the word. "Go ahead. Fulfill what you've always wanted to do. I'm here, alone. There's no one to protect me. You're big and strong. Think about what your powerful hands would feel like around my throat, stopping my voice forever."

"No!"

"Then I'll haunt you forever, you'll never be free of me...."

Something in him snapped, and he rushed at her, bellowing like a bull. He reached out for her, but her body was light as air, insubstantial as a candle flame. But there was something... a living throat, blood pulsing in the arteries... and he caught at it, held on, squeezed until the breath stopped and the last feeble shudderings of life slipped away, groaning, into the shadows of the Arizona night.

• • •

Reverend Zedekiah Collins knelt near the crumpled figure collapsed in the dusty street, holding a lantern aloft to shine light on the face.

"Lord save us," said Mort Cavanaugh, his voice hushed. "It's Dan Robichaux."

"I heard him call out," Reverend Collins said. "Couldn't make out any words. I came out here as soon as I could, but it was too late. Whoever killed him had already fled."

"Maybe it was revenge," Jeb Mitchell said. "Word was, he was a murderer on the run. Had killed some poor girl back in his home town, and run off to avoid the gallows."

Collins nodded. "He came to my room tonight, only a short time ago. He wanted to see my daughter. He may have had the idea that she knew the girl he killed. He certainly seemed mad."

Cavanaugh shook his head. "Poor blighter. He seemed normal enough until a few days ago. Until a woman showed up and started telling everyone what he'd done. Wonder if maybe she's the sister of the girl he killed? Maybe she's the one who did this, you think?"

"No way to tell," Reverend Collins said. "And if he was a murderer, maybe it's for the best. The Lord works in mysterious ways."

Cavanaugh and Mitchell nodded.

"It's weird," Mitchell said, peering down at Dan Robichaux's still body, "from the look of it, his hands were around his own throat. Look at the bruises on his neck. Weren't no girl's hands did that."

Reverend Collins shrugged. "Whoever did it, it's clear to me that justice was served." He straightened up. "Now someone go get the sheriff."

. . .

Sara Collins pulled a comb through her long copper hair, and put a modest lace cap over it, making sure that enough was visible to be alluring. Her father was gone, off to a meeting of the San Diego Temperance Society, and wouldn't be back until late. It gave her plenty of time for a long walk, and ample opportunity to do what she liked best, which was simultaneously excite and frustrate the attentions of any local boys who happened to be around. A little smile playing around her lips, she walked down the stairs of the sleeping quarters of the Mission San Diego de Alcala, where she and her father had been given rooms.

San Diego was certainly a more pleasant place than Safford, Arizona. Cooler, more verdant, and most importantly, more people. Safford was too new and too raw for her father's message to take root, and was boring and desolate for her.

And the events that had taken place the night they arrived were unpleasant memories, the stuff of nightmares. Best to get away from them, forget them, pretend they never happened.

It was as she turned a corner toward the center of town that she saw him, a tall, broad-shouldered man in a scuffed shirt and pants that had seen years of hard use. The sleeves were rolled up to the elbow, revealing powerfully-muscled forearms. His boots clunked hollowly on the hard surface of the road as he approached. His face was dark, with a swatch of black hair coming from underneath a broad-brimmed hat that shadowed his eyes.

Sara's heart beat a little faster. Maybe it would have been better to stay in the room at the Mission, as she'd promised her father. Maybe going into town in the evening wasn't safe. Who knew what kind of men she'd run into? What their intentions were? What secrets lay in their past?

The man slowed as he came near her. She caught a glimpse of dark eyes glittering underneath the hat brim. He stopped in front of her.

"Sara Collins?" he said, in a grim tone.

"Yes?" she said, trying to keep her voice light, and not let the cold hand of fear that clenched her heart stop her tongue. "Do I know you?"

"No," he said. "But I know you."

She opened her mouth to answer, but no words came out.

He leaned forward, till she could feel the warmth from his body, smell the whiskey on his breath.

"And I know what you are."

Gordon Bonnet

Gordon Bonnet has been writing fiction for decades. Encouraged when his story *Crazy Bird Bends His Beak* won critical acclaim in Mrs. Moore's 1st grade class at Central Elementary School in St. Albans, West Virginia, he embarked on a love affair with the written word.

His interest in the paranormal goes back almost that far. Introduced to speculative, fantasy, and science fiction by such giants in the tradition as Madeleine L'Engle, Isaac Asimov, C. S. Lewis, and J. R. R. Tolkien, he was captivated by those writers' abilities to take the reader to a fictional world and make it seem tangible, to breathe life and passion and personality into characters who were (sometimes) not even human. He made journeys into darker realms upon meeting the works of Edgar Allen Poe and H. P. Lovecraft during his teenage years, and those authors still influence his imagination and his writing to this day.

This fascination with the paranormal, however, has always been tempered by Gordon's scientific training. This has led to a strange duality—his work as a skeptic on the popular blog *Skeptophilia,* while simultaneously writing speculative novels and short stories. He explains this, with a smile: "Well, I do know it's fiction, after all." He blogs daily, and is never without a piece of fiction in progress.

you don't see *that* EVERY DAY

Darrel Sparkman
western columnist

I never put myself out there as any kind of gun expert—old time or new. However, I know what I like to shoot and see a lot of stuff in pursuit of the western/frontier/apocalyptic, and contemporary novel. I get surprised once in a while.

It's not your normal pellet gun or BB gun. Some firearms you just use and never think about their origin. I have an air rifle that I like a lot. It's not your normal pellet gun or BB gun. It's a break-barrel Gamo Whisper with a scope and suppressor (sort-of). Now this sweet little gun pops out a .177 pellet and 1275 feet per second. For a rough comparison, my trusty old .22 long rifle travels at roughly 1200 feet per second. Yeah, I know the bullet is heavier and it has more power behind it—but, you get the idea. To hit a target fifty to a hundred feet away with a pellet half the size of a pea (Little Marvel or Snow King for those with their caliper out) is no easy endeavor, but it's easy with the right air rifle.

Imagine my surprise when I read that the Lewis and Clark expedition, circa 1804, used an air rifle. Ok, my feeble mind tried to wrap itself around that tidbit. Was it kind of like my air rifle? Knock down the occasional rabbit or squirrel? Oh, I don't think so.

The Girandoni air rifle was the real deal. Designed by Bartholomaus Girandoni (we'd call him Bart around here) around 1779, the Germans called it a wind rifle—and no, I won't go there. The Austrian army used this thing until around 1815, before they scrapped it for more reliable weapons that go *boom* instead of *pffft*. Napoleon sure didn't like it used against him. It is said he ordered the execution of any soldier caught with one.

For those who think it might've been a toy, think of this. Capable of firing 20 shots as fast as they could work a little lever and drop another ball into the firing chamber. I'm thinking one shot every five seconds would be a good number—compared to about one a minute by a very good operator with any of the muzzleloaders or other contemporary firearm. Think of this—a person with one of these rifles firing fifteen shots a minute (I'm sure that number is very arbitrary) could be devastating to any attacking force, especially in the rain or snow when it's hard to "keep your powder dry." And, it came with extra air chambers that could be changed very quickly. Not charged quickly, but changed.

How powerful? It would shoot a .46 caliber ball through a one-inch pine board at 100 yards. However, with each shot, the power would drop. After about 20 shots you might as well start throwing lead balls by hand, or start running.

Unfortunately, this instrument needed a lot of care and support system. The slightest ding in the air bladder could cause it to lose air, and the leather seals were prone to drying up and not working. It also took about 1500 cycles with a pump, similar to a bicycle pump, to fill the chamber. Imagine having the bad guys coming over the wall with you holding up your hand and yelling, "Hang on, guys. I'll be with you in just a minute. Only got 500 pumps to go." No, not good.

I won't go into all the technical aspects of this gun, but if you're interested, look it up. It's fascinating reading. There's a lot of supposition about how the gun was used by Meriwether Lewis, but anything is possible.

There are also many powerful air rifles on the market today that can be used in large game hunting—deer, wild boar, and buffalo were mentioned.

Detail of the removable air bladder in the stock of the Girandoni Air Rifle. The slightest ding could cause it to lose air, and the leather seals were prone to drying up. It also took about 1500 cycles with a device similar to a bicycle pump, to fill the chamber.

One thing to consider. In the forests of the frontier 1800s, or in an apocalyptic world in the future, the key to survival is silence. You don't want anyone to know where you are or that you exist, especially when you're hunting for food. So, if you're trying to pull a sneaky Pete, slinking through the landscape, high tech bow and arrow notwithstanding—would you rather have something that goes *Boom* or *pffft?*

That's all for now.

—Darrel Sparkman resides in Missouri with his wife. He served four years in the Navy, including seven months in Viet Nam as a combat search & rescue helicopter crewman. His new column, You Don't See That Everyday, will be a regular addition to Saddlebag Dispatches, and explore some of the more unique and whimsical things to be found in Wild West history.

John E. Biggs

AWARD-WINNING AUTHOR

JOHNBIGGSOKLAHOMAWRITER.COM

ONE LAST IMAGE

VELDA BROTHERTON
Author of *Montana Promises*

Papa shook her shoulder. "It's time to go, Allie. Be quiet so as not to wake Mama and the girls. We've said our goodbyes."

Fire crackled to life in the fireplace and her breath misted in the cold air when she peered from beneath the pile of quilts. Dawn lay in silver bars across the pinewood floor and outside the rooster crowed in the stillness. The water bucket would be froze this morning.

Was she really doing this? Her heart hammered so she could hardly draw a breath. She and Papa going to the battlefields to make photographs. One day all the world would look at them, or so he claimed. That didn't keep her from being scared. Yet it was too late to back out even if she wanted to. And she didn't. It would be the greatest and most romantic adventure of her life. Maybe she would meet a handsome soldier and fall in love. It was high time.

Mama had cried and begged her not to go. Bess and Meg followed suit. All pleaded with Papa to change his mind, to stay home and let that dreadful war play out without him, but the die was cast.

He grumped right back in his stern voice. "She's a woman grown, turned seventeen. I'll not let any harm come to her. It's not as if we will be in battle. Photographs are made in the aftermath while the subjects remain still. Had Mama produced a son, he would go. But she didn't. It's up to our Allie. Now hush, all of you."

And they had stopped complaining because he would brook no disobedience. He was a firm task master, having taught his eldest child all the principles of photography, despite the unfortunate fact she was not a boy.

She lowered her feet to the cold floor, curled her toes, and dressed quickly in the manner a son would dress. Britches, itchy linsey-woolsey shirt, gaiters, and thick knit socks. Her dressing like that disturbed Mama but Papa would have it no other way. Carrying her brogans, she followed Papa to the front door and sat on the steps beside him to pull them on. They gathered their bags and crossed the yard to the barn where the what's-it wagon and horse awaited. Purple Ozark hills rolled into the distance against the lightening sky, the February morning still and cold as blue blazes.

She shivered, gathered the leathers, and hooked Rex onto the single tree with stiff fingers while Papa placed their bags in the back, taking great care in the loading. The wagon carried their glass plates and all the chemicals along with the new wet plate camera and tripod purchased the month before when the decision to go had been reached.

She climbed onto the wagon seat. He followed, settled, gathered the reins, and slapped Rex's rump. The sky was light enough to make out the house and barn, the corral fence, and an outline of the well. Over her shoulder home faded out of sight to the thudding of the horse's hooves along the road that led toward an unknown fate. Fear she might never see her mama and sisters again clutched her stomach like a giant fist. Did she really want to do this? Yes. No. Of course. But still....

Late that day they arrived in Westport. Noise filled the busy city streets where wagons pulled by mules and horses and riders on horseback churned up the mud. The stench filled her nostrils, and breathing through her mouth brought on a coughing fit. Papa left her with the wagon and soon returned with the latest about the war.

It wasn't till he finished loading grain for Rex and supplies for the trail that he climbed up and shared what he'd learned.

"End of last year, Federals took a sound beating down to Stones River." Since the beginning Papa had been a staunch supporter of the Confederacy, so he relished the defeat of the hated enemy.

He reined Rex out of the way of a large freight wagon, then went on. "Don't mean plenty of our boys didn't die. Blood was shed on both sides, but we gave a sound beating." He shook his head. "Not so good, though, down to Arkansas Post. Them bluecoats wiped out thousands of Confederates in a three-day battle, while keeping their own losses low. Not near as bloody as Stones River, yet it spelled a terrible defeat for the Rebs. That was back in January, and nothing much by the way of news has come through since then."

On the edge of town, at the wagon yard, he pulled in and they settled in a spot for overnight. Allie would rather have camped on the trail, but Papa preferred this place.

"Just stay quiet and out of sight. We'll sleep under the wagon and be on our way in the morning."

Behind the wagon he built a small fire from wood supplied by the yard owner for two-bits and they cooked beans and made coffee. She liked to never got to sleep for all the noise and wahooing along the street plus the music coming from a nearby bar with the unbelievable name of The Mule Shoe. Papa returned from the place and settled into his bedroll before she finally dropped off.

The next day they were on their way south, with her relieved to be out in the countryside where one could draw a clean breath. Occasionally she imagined sounds of gunfire and screams of agony from a distant battlefield, but it was only in her head. Despite her excitement the days and nights soon grew monotonous and sleeping on the ground changed from an adventure to just plain uncomfortable. Late one afternoon a man in a tattered gray uniform toting a musket trudged toward them. Head down, he stumbled on past as if they were not there. A bloody bandage covered his head. An image far from the ones she had imagined before beginning the trip. Papa didn't greet the man or stop and set up the camera to take his picture. She didn't ask why. Didn't want to know.

Another day, weary and sore from setting on that blamed wagon seat day in and day out, she inquired of Papa, "How far is it to the war?"

"Just over the next hill." He clicked his tongue at Rex and said no more.

She worked her hat down tighter. The day before they left home he'd taken a pair of shears and cut her long walnut-colored hair till it shagged around her ears like the boy she was supposed to be. Again Mama cried. She cried a lot those last few days before they left. Papa remained sour as if he'd bit into an unripe persimmon. Yet when he hugged and kissed Mama goodbye that night he cradled the back of her head in his palm for a long time.

The war was not over the next hill, nor the next. Just endless coils of dirt roads and once in a while dust devils blown up by gusting wind. By then she walked alongside the wagon a portion of each day to stretch the aching muscles.

On a late afternoon, right out of the blue, Papa called Rex to halt. Daydreams of handsome men in uniform mounted on white horses carried her away and she didn't see a body lying in the ditch beside the road until they rolled to a halt.

"Stay here, girl. Don't you move." He wrapped the reins around the brake handle and jumped down.

Of course, she leaped right down on her side, spied what was there, and wished she hadn't. The body lay on one arm, his other twisted behind him as if broken. On his hip was strapped a revolver, fancy pearl handle gleaming in the pale light. He wore a blue uniform, smeared with blood and mud.

She pinched her mouth shut, then immediately opened it to vomit. Papa must've heard, for he whirled, pointed a finger at her.

"Git yourself back up on that seat this minute. You got no business staring at this. And you stay there."

For a few minutes she kept her eyes squeezed tight shut until it came clear that Papa had gone to the back of the wagon and climbed in. After a bit he hopped down and his footsteps gritted alongside the road. She looked, she had to. Couldn't help it. He was setting up the camera at an angle to the body.

"Papa, no." She screamed, the noise sending blackbirds exploding out of a nearby sycamore. The man in the ditch moved and she screamed again.

"Dang it, girl. Turn away and mind your business."

Sobs jerked in her chest. "He's not dead. He's *not!* Can't we help him?"

Papa moved away from the camera, knelt down next to the soldier, spread a hand on his neck. After a moment he shook his head, and his hand inched toward the pearl handle.

No, Papa. No, don't do that. Though her mouth opened nothing came out. Why didn't he stop? He was going to take that gun and nothing she could do about it. Her heart was going to strangle her, it beat so hard in her throat.

Suppose he shot that man dead, right there? To keep from watching, she stared out across the valley on the other side of the road. After a while he returned to the wagon, climbed up on the seat, and smacked Rex on the rump with the reins.

Over the next few days she thought about that revolver. She'd never seen him touch a gun before. Had he this time? If he did, she hadn't seen it. And he didn't shoot that poor dying man, just left him there. How dreadful. Oh, dear. If he did take it, what was he planning on doing with it?

One day he asked her to recite the chemicals and the way they would be used to wet the glass plates and make the photographs. Because learning from him was like playing a complicated game that she dared not get wrong lest she suffer his scowl, she recited the proper order of chemicals. And she did, making a little song out of it.

"Treat with collodion, in the dark silver nitrate, expose for image, back in the dark use pyrogallic acid, then wash with water, varnish to finish, and it's ready to print." Games like that did help make the time go by.

The creaking wheels carried them closer and closer to what she imagined might be the war. Somewhere in Tennessee there was gunfire from around a curve ahead. Papa halted Rex out of sight under a bluff that hung over the narrow road. A spring ran from between the rocks making a small rushing sound. With a finger over his lips he motioned her to get down. He didn't have to shush her. She wouldn't dare make a noise and be noticed by all those men firing guns and shouting at each other.

At the rear of the wagon, he climbed in and handed down the tripod and heavy wooden camera.

Oh, no. He was going to make photographs of a real gunfight with lead flying and people getting killed. He'd said they would not be in battle. He must've just told Mama that so she wouldn't worry. Maybe he wouldn't ask her to help.

When he climbed into the wagon, his coat flapped open to reveal the pearl-handled revolver strapped to his waist.

What was he going to do? Go in shooting. One look at that gun and those men killing each other were bound to shoot him. She couldn't bear the idea, but it was no use saying anything. Papa would do as he pleased.

The flap came down behind him, creating a darkroom in the back so he could prepare the glass plate. After a moment he stepped out with a thin wooden box and slid it in the camera. He slipped the box out, leaving the plate in place. When he wanted to make a photograph he would hunch behind the camera under the black canvas, aim the lens at his subject, and remove its cover for a few seconds. The image would be transferred to the glass plate, making it ready to develop onto paper. Plenty of water was needed for the washing process, thus the stop near a stream. The beauty of such a thing never ceased to amaze her, yet she couldn't stop thinking about that gun on his hip.

Shaking with fear, she hunkered on the far side of the wagon under the bluff where the soldiers couldn't see her. The echoing shots sounded like popcorn popping. The spring gurgled. A smell of damp earth and black powder tickled her nostrils. What if they killed each other? All of them? What if Papa used the pearl-handled revolver to shoot them?

Making a photograph of dead bodies never occurred to

her while he was teaching her to become a photographer. Maybe she didn't want to after all.

At last a long silence ensued and it appeared the men were done shooting at each other. Black smoke drifted upward and away. Papa took up the camera, signaled to her to bring the tripod.

"And stay directly behind me. You understand?"

Boots kicking up puffs of dust, he walked down the middle of that road and around the curve straight onto the battlefield. Knees shaking till she could barely walk, she did her best to stay right behind him like he'd ordered, but it was hard to stretch her short legs and place her footsteps exactly in his. Her tongue dried up, stuck to the roof of her mouth. Fear became a live, wriggling thing hung in her throat. What if the soldiers turned and shot them?

Papa waved a white handkerchief and hollered. "Hey there, fellas. I'd like to make a photograph of you, if you don't mind."

Relieved that he didn't pull out the revolver, she peered around him at five men standing in the middle of the road, all staring toward her and Papa, each wearing the blue coat of the terrible Federal Army. Her and Papa were sure to get shot by those Yankee devils. Everyone knew how brutal they were. They'd already killed, for several bodies lay on the ground. Only one was a bluecoat. A fallen butternut raised onto his elbows and groaned, another had blood all over his head and rolled around in the dirt crying for his mama. Two more lay deathly still. Poor southern boys hadn't had a chance. Murdered. Probably shot in the back if the truth were known.

What if Papa had been shot? Killed dead and then they would have taken her, learned she wasn't a boy but a woman. Then what? She shuddered to think what.

Four of the five bluecoats strutted forward, each placed a foot on a fallen butternut to pose for Papa. The butts of their rifles rested on the ground, their eyes stared from dirty faces. The fifth man turned and limped off as if he'd maybe been shot in the leg. She couldn't take it anymore. Scared as she was, something had to be done.

Without further thought of her own danger, she leaped in front of Papa, not caring that she ruined his photograph. "You all ought to be ashamed of yourselves. Killing those poor boys, then posing like you'd brought down some animals or something."

"Allie Mae Caine, you hush your mouth and come back behind me this minute. I want to thank you men for posing for me." His tone was so formal she barely escaped screaming at him, but that wasn't allowed. Never had been. She ground her teeth, fists clenched into the folds of her britches. The murdering devils.

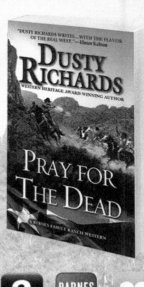

Oh, my goodness. Papa had called her by her girl name. Now those devils knew she was a woman. They'd probably ravage her right there in the road. It was definitely time to hightail it back to safety in the wagon. Time for Papa to show that gun so they could get out of there.

"You want another pitcher, we'll stand for it." The shortest of the dreadful soldiers kept his place amid the bodies.

"No, that's okay. I apologize for the trouble. We'll just be on our way." Papa grabbed up the camera, still attached to the tripod, and hurried to follow Allie to the wagon. A murmur went through the group, then one of the bluecoats hollered.

"Be careful, mister. These woods is filled with bushwhackers. They'll kill you for the pure fun of it." Without another word they turned and shuffled away.

For a long moment, she stood where she had hidden, shaking so hard she could hear her teeth rattle. A strange silence settled around her like a day at a funeral after all the hymns have been sung and thinking about that corpse in the coffin. What had just happened? They'd almost got killed by those bluecoats, that's what. At the back of the wagon, she swallowed fast to keep from gagging. Stared up into Papa's angry features.

"I'm sorry, I truly am." Her voice came out so tiny she didn't think he heard her.

"I hope that's a lesson learned, girl. A wonder they didn't just shoot us down. Possible they didn't have their guns loaded after the scrimmage. You must learn to keep your mouth shut."

She nodded. "I will. I will."

"Your fear is enough punishment. Now crawl up there and let's be on our way. Next time you'll know better."

He never once mentioned that he'd revealed her being a girl and what might have happened. Probably never would either.

Once in the seat, she couldn't keep from asking, "Aren't they even going to bury the bodies?"

"Probably not. But some more Rebs will come along and do it. That or predators will clean their bones. It's a pitiful thing, dying like that. But we are born to die, child. Properly when we're old and used up, not like these boys. It seems of no real use, but maybe we need to look death in the eye to appreciate life." He shook his head and stared at the dead soldiers. "If the South don't put this to rest and soon, it'll kill us. Kill us for generations."

"I've decided that I don't approve of war at all, and I'll never understand why men go out and kill each other. I don't know why you make pictures of dead men."

"If someone doesn't record the worst of life, how do we live the best? These men died for what they believed in. Some die for each other. For love of their wives, brothers, sisters, parents, friends. Their sacrifice should not go for naught. It's

LOSING
COTTON

A NOVEL

J.B. HOGAN

to record the bloody brutality of war that we will make these photographs. Maybe everyone will remember longer."

His voice grew angry, or perhaps stern was a better word. It might be a long time before she stopped shaking. Sorry that she'd upset him, she stared out across the mountains, tipped in gold by the setting sun. It was time to make camp for the night. She still couldn't ask him what he meant to do with the revolver.

The aroma of boiling coffee surrounded the small camp, set off the trail a good ways and surrounded by woods. Firelight sent the naked branches into a macabre dance and she snuggled tighter into her blankets, remembering the warning of the bluecoat. There'd been some reports of bushwhackers up in Missouri, but none had ever hit the small town of Salem that she knew of.

She and Papa had finished their meal when the men rushed out of the night so fast there wasn't time to run or fight. One rough voice ordered them to stay right where they were.

And she did, she surely did. Sat straight up and tucked the horse-smelling blanket under her chin. Probably those Yankees circled around and now they were going to kill her and Papa. Eyes wide, she tried to see Papa in the dying firelight. Only shadows moved around so she couldn't tell him from the intruders. As afraid of what he would do as what was about to happen, she hugged herself and shivered.

When the shot rang out, shouts followed and she feared what had happened. Feared it deep in her bones. Don't look, don't think. Then her fears wouldn't be proved true.

"Crazy old codger, what'd he do that fer?"

A voice she didn't know coming from beyond the fire so she couldn't see. But she knew. Oh, dear Lord she knew. She threw back the blanket, scrambled on hands and knees in the dirt toward where she'd last seen Papa.

Whimpering, crying out, she didn't make it all the way before rough hands snatched her up off the ground like she was a sack of feed.

"Let me go, you blue devil. Turn me loose." All the fighting and screaming did no good.

"Stay back, son. You cain't do nothing fer him. Pulled a gun on me, he did. No one needed to get hurt." He tossed her down to the ground. "Now stay put and nothing will happen to you. We're just wanting your horse and food. You kin keep that dumb looking wagon. No use fer it."

She came up shouting, threw herself at him when he turned away. Hit waist high, the outlaw staggered to his knees. Another came from behind her.

"Give me a holt of that youngun, I'll show him how to best behave." He grabbed her under both arms, fingers spreading over her breasts.

"Well, now. What in thunder do we have here, men? Guess what old Foley has found?" He poked at her breasts. "This here feller is a she-male. What do you think of that?"

"Stop. You stop it." She slapped his hands away. "Where's my papa? What'd you do to him?"

"Shut up fore you wakes the dead." He hit her hard in the chest with the flat of his hand, sent her tumbling.

From the different voices and shadows darting around, there must be at least three men. She needed to get to Papa, but this time no noise. While the outlaws pawed through their meager belongings, she crawled toward the still form that had to be Papa. Maybe he wasn't dead. Hand on his shoulder, she rolled him over, whispered to him. He didn't move or speak. Heart breaking, she lay her ear on his chest but could hear nothing. With one palm, she checked to see if he was breathing. Still nothing.

Lips next to his ear, she whispered through teary sobs, "Papa, don't be dead. Please don't be dead." She shook his shoulder. "Wake up now, you hear me? You have to wake up." But he didn't.

Fury grew so huge she couldn't contain it. They had killed Papa. She would make them pay. Sobbing till she could barely see or take a breath, she clawed open his coat to search for the revolver. Maybe he wasn't really dead. She patted on either side. She wasn't a doctor. Where was it? Had he taken it off earlier? Pockets. Nothing but his watch. Did he take a breath? She shook him.

"Papa. Papa." Whispered so they wouldn't hear. Maybe it was in his bedroll.

Someone grabbed her by the back of her shirt, one strong arm fastened around her middle.

"No, stop it. Wait. I have to see if he's alive. Let me go." Her flailing feet contacted flesh and bone. The man howled. A fist boxed her on the side of the head. Everything went black.

Voices, chattering, laughing. She grunted when she was tossed over the back of a horse. The steady plodding sent pain through her. Tears burned her nose and throat.

"Hold up there." A shout from off to the side.

Who was that? What was happening?

"Drop your weapons and get her down off that horse."

Her hands were tied together over her head, ankles the same. Still she squirmed and fought. Shouted. "Help me, please."

A shot rang out. Her captors shouted. Another shot. Both from the darkness where the voice called from.

"Okay, mister. I give up. You can quit killing us." That was one of the outlaws. Someone had come to save her.

"Get down off your horse. Untie her and set her on her feet."

Hands worked at her ankles, then unfastened the knots around her wrists, slid her to the ground where she landed with a thunk.

"Now you ride on out. No, leave those horses." Someone knelt beside her. "You okay?"

A horse galloped off into the night.

"Papa. They killed my papa."

"I'm sorry. I couldn't get here sooner. They—uh—sorry."

A noise, like he fell to the ground. She crawled toward the sound, bumped into a sprawled figure. One of the men he'd shot? She patted along his side. He groaned.

"What is it? Who are you?"

"I'm wounded. Your papa took our picture earlier."

THE LONG AND SHORT OF IT.

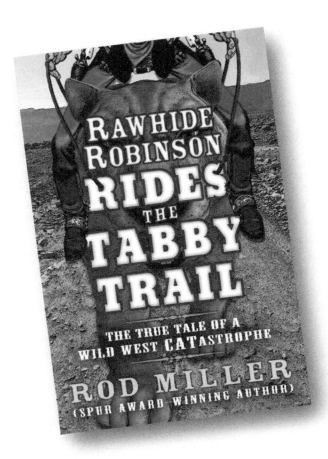

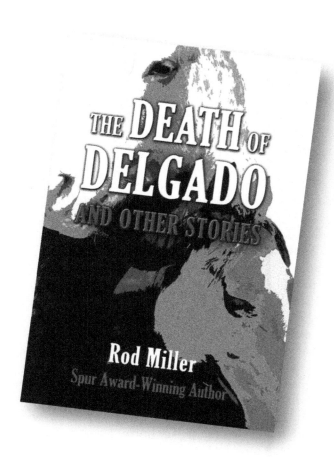

RAWHIDE ROBINSON RIDES THE TABBY TRAIL: THE TRUE TALE OF A WILD WEST CATASTROPHE finds ordinary cowboy Rawhide Robinson once again in the middle of extraordinary adventures in this 252-page novel. On a one-of-a-kind CATtle drive to Tombstone to relieve a plague of rats, he regales the crew with wild and wooly Western tales.

ISBN 978-1-4328-3075-5 Five Star

THE DEATH OF DELGADO AND OTHER STORIES gathers twenty head of short stories, including the Western Writers of America Spur Award-winning title tale and a Spur Award Finalist. The West, old and new, is the setting for this collection of short stories that cover a wide range in style and subject, from traditional to unconventional.

ISBN 978-1-942428-54-1 Pen-L Publishing

"One of the bluecoats? A Yankee?"

He cleared his throat. Tried to speak some more. Couldn't.

Why would a Federal bother to save her? Weren't they supposed to be the ones on the wrong side in this war? The hated enemy? The blue devils?

She found his hand, took it in hers. He squeezed her fingers. "Mister, are you okay?"

"Wife. Tell her I spoke of her… at the end. Will you?" He let go, his body relaxing under her touch.

No reply. No sound of breathing. It was too much, way too much. She slumped beside his body for a long time, afraid she might never stop crying. This war, this dreadful war. Taking Papa, then this man, an enemy, who died saving her. A man whose name she did not know. Someone who had a wife who would grieve his passing, yet never know where or how.

Cold seeped into her body. Nearby a horse whickered, then a soft nose nudged her bare cheek. She pushed to a sitting position, struggled to her feet. A half-moon peeked from behind a drift of clouds to light the night. The soldier who had saved her lay on his back, hands folded across his chest, eyes open staring at nothing. He wore the blue uniform of a Federal. Two other bodies lay a few feet away.

Again tears. She fell down beside him. "I'm sorry. I'm so sorry."

Too hard to voice all the things she was sorry for. Papa killed, her hatred of the very man who had saved her life, herself for being alone. Would she ever get back home, and when she did how would she tell Mama and the girls about Papa and all that had happened?

She ought to see if the Yankee had his name in his pockets somewhere. It was important to know who he was before she went back to see to Papa. Though she wasn't exactly sure why, she searched his pockets till she found a carte de visite of a lovely woman. Written on the cardboard frame were the words, "to Lyle with love, Mary."

On her knees, she touched his cheek, already going cold. "Thank you, Lyle. I'm sorry, so sorry." He didn't appear like an enemy lying there so cold, so dead.

Taking up the reins of the horse she took the time to hitch him to the wagon. Too tired to climb up on the seat, she led him toward the flickering remnants of the campfire her and Papa had built what seemed like an eternity ago. She felt old, like maybe a lot of years had passed. And before this night ended, with what she had yet to do, she would feel a lot older still.

One thing for sure. She would finish what Papa had started, much as she hated the idea, and when this war was over, she would go west. Somewhere where blood didn't stain the land. A place where she could make a new start.

Velda Brotherton

Velda Brotherton writes from her home perched on the side of a mountain against the Ozark National Forest. Branded as *Sexy, Dark and Gritty,* her work embraces the lives of gutsy women and heroes who are strong enough to deserve them. After a stint writing for a New York publisher, she has settled comfortably in with small publishers to produce novels in several genres.

Velda's latest works include three romantic mysteries from her dark and steamy Twist of Poe Series—*The Purloined Skull, The Tell-Tale Stone,* and *The Pit and the Penance*—the mainstream love story *Beyond the Moon,* the erotic horror novel *A Savage Grace,* and The Victorians, a Western Historical Romance series including the novels *Wilda's Outlaw* and *Rowena's Hellion.* She is a founding member of the Northwest Arkansas Writers' Workshop and Storytellers of America, Ozark Original Chapter, as well as a member of Ozark Creative Writers, Women Writing the West, Western Writers of America, and the Oklahoma Writers' Federation, Inc.

WELCOME TO
REDWOOD
COUNTRY

I n 1864 when Merritt Curtis Foster rode into town, Eureka, California was the westernmost point in the United States. I've always believed Great-great-great Grandpa Merritt had the good sense to flee Coffee County, Kansas to avoid participation in the Civil War. Whatever brought Grandpa to this land of dense redwoods, thick fog, and abundant rain, my family has lived on the shores of Humboldt Bay ever since.

We have stories. . .

STORY & PHOTOS BY
PAMELA FOSTER

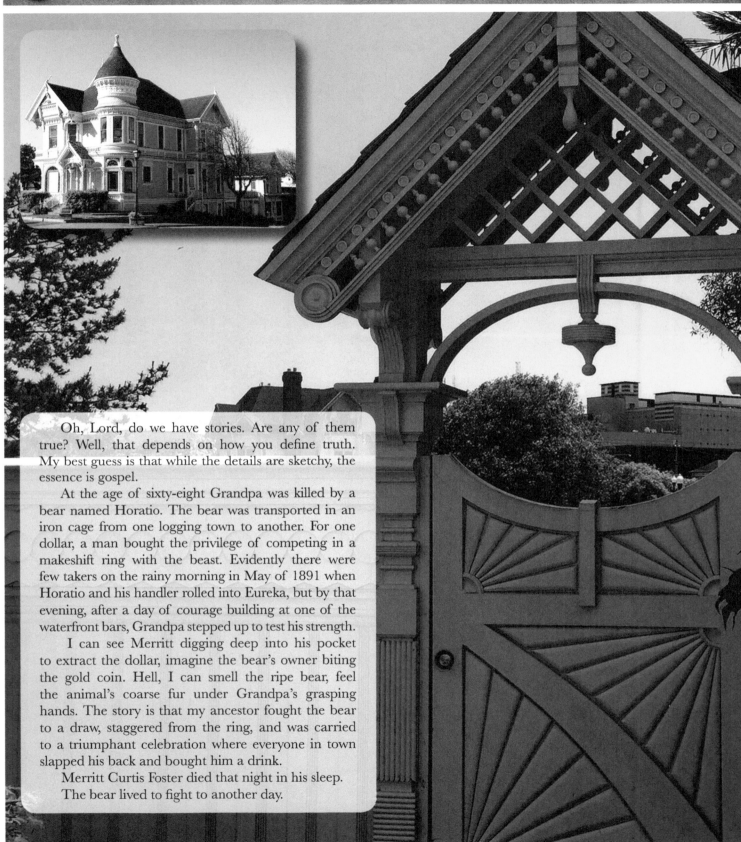

Oh, Lord, do we have stories. Are any of them true? Well, that depends on how you define truth. My best guess is that while the details are sketchy, the essence is gospel.

At the age of sixty-eight Grandpa was killed by a bear named Horatio. The bear was transported in an iron cage from one logging town to another. For one dollar, a man bought the privilege of competing in a makeshift ring with the beast. Evidently there were few takers on the rainy morning in May of 1891 when Horatio and his handler rolled into Eureka, but by that evening, after a day of courage building at one of the waterfront bars, Grandpa stepped up to test his strength.

I can see Merritt digging deep into his pocket to extract the dollar, imagine the bear's owner biting the gold coin. Hell, I can smell the ripe bear, feel the animal's coarse fur under Grandpa's grasping hands. The story is that my ancestor fought the bear to a draw, staggered from the ring, and was carried to a triumphant celebration where everyone in town slapped his back and bought him a drink.

Merritt Curtis Foster died that night in his sleep. The bear lived to fight to another day.

Charming garden gate on the victorian home known as The Pink Lady near downtown Eureka.

The eighteen room, two-and-a-half story Carson Mansion built by timber baron William Carson between 1884 and 1885. Now known as the Ingomar Club, the mansion housed an exclusive men's club for years.

Then there was Aunt Mandy who, from 1920 to 1933 when prohibition ended, ran a brothel on Second Street. We have stories galore about Mandy. I grew up hearing about her monkey fur coat, a gift from Tom Mix. When I was much younger, I evidently looked like Mandy and would occasionally be approached by old men who, with a tear, or perhaps a cataract magnified twinkle in their eye, told me I reminded them of someone from their youth. When they learned my last name, these men always, just for a moment, looked forty years younger.

Perhaps you sense a theme in these family stories. My family is more rough and ready than cultured and civilized. But then, in Humboldt County there is far more call for the former than for the latter.

The Vance Hotel where family legend says Aunt Mandy entertained the likes of Tom Mix.

Sequioa Park and the Sequioa Park Zoo just south of Eureka are both filled with the many natural wonders that make Redwood Country such a sought-after tourist destination.

The Riverwalk in nearby Fortuna, California, a great place for walking and reflecting while surrounded by beautiful natural vistas like it was on this particular afternoon.

Eureka has always been nearly impossible to get to. Even today, slides across highways and general bad weather and poor infrastructure keep all but the most determined from visiting. Humboldt County, with Eureka at its center, sits quietly behind the redwood curtain, shrouded in fog, nestled in the tall trees, and cradled between the coastal range and the Pacific Ocean. Unemployment is twice the national average and underemployment rampant. My ancestors cut the forest and over-fished the ocean and rivers and lagoons. Their descendants do their best to make ends meet.

The chamber of commerce will tell you tourism is our biggest industry, and people do indeed arrive from all over the world to see this beautiful place. These folks bitch about how difficult it was to get here, are frightened by our resident homeless population, stroll a few feet in a redwood forest, walk along a beach and go back to where they earn twice or three times what our locals make while paying half the rent or mortgage.

But the economic lifeblood of the county is marijuana. Good ole boys have a license to grow ten plants and harvest a couple hundred. Cartels have moved in. Once clear streams and rivers are poisoned with fertilizer runoff. Home invasions of small growers is common. Trimmers arrive by the hundreds at harvest time, stay to join the local homeless at food banks and on street corners, or disappear into the mountains never to be seen again.

Times have changed since Great-great-great Grandpa wrestled Horatio, or Aunt Mandy entertained Tom Mix. The fishy smell of the bay at low tide still mingles with wet redwood, feathery anise, and the thick muck of ferns and dirt forever wet. But now days, marijuana smoke often overlays these scents. Still, if I concentrate, I can smell the tang of a wrestling bear, feel the burn of bootleg whiskey, hear the soft call of home.

—Pamela Foster is the award-winning author of five novels, two nonfiction books, and numerous short stories and essays. While she has traveled the world in the company of her Vietnam-veteran husband, she has recently gone back to her roots and returned to her beloved hometown of Eureka, California.

JC CRUMPTON

G MEN

PART TWO

"Y ou sure they came this way, Marshal?" Jerome looked up at the oak and black walnut trees covering the small hill north of Baxter Springs.

Thick clouds kept the moon hidden, and their torches and one bullhorn lantern could not penetrate the thick darkness of the grove. Deep blackness hung in the spaces between the trees like shadows wrapped up inside more shadows. The rain earlier had even sent the tree frogs into hiding, and only the plop of fat drops falling from the trees onto the ground reached his ears.

The marshal's lantern bobbed as he nodded, sending the beam of light raking up and down the front edge of the forest.

"They must have." The light settled. "It's the surest route out of town heading toward Abner's place, and they weren't there. They don't have anywhere else to go except here."

"Do you trust this witness at the Diamond Hotel?" Rondal kept his gaze on the forest hilltop above them and clucked his tongue against the back of his teeth.

Jerome bit his bottom lip and wondered what his brother could be thinking. Some thought or plan would be whirling about in the man's head, mulling over some strategy. Where Jerome liked to get things done, Rondal often deliberated for days on the simplest of decisions. The only thing was—Jerome had to admit to himself—Rondal usually had the better ideas. But this time they didn't have the luxury of reflection. Zeke and their father needed justice to be done as quickly as possible.

"I don't know why I shouldn't." Jerome looked over at the marshal. The man's hat cast shadows deep enough that he could not tell if the man frowned or not when he answered. The flickering lights from the torches he and his brother held aloft cast surging areas of light around them that pulsed like an erratic heartbeat, illuminating little more than the area around them before being swallowed up by more of the gloom and repeating the process.

Shrugging, Jerome turned back toward the hilltop and nudged his horse forward. "I just don't know how far I could trust a man that wore a top hat out here. They always seem to be some carpetbagger intent on cheating people out of their hard-earned properties."

Beside him, Rondal grunted. "That's not what I meant, Jerome." A brief silence followed his words, long enough that Jerome started to twist around in his saddle only for Rondal to

continue. "I was wondering if this man had any business connections to anyone in town, and if any of those connections had any association with Abner or his nephew."

"Oh." Jerome pulled his horse to a stop and waited for the other two to come up beside him.

When the other two halted their own mounts, Jerome looked over at Marshal Baker's shadow-covered face. The man's head slowly shook back and forth. "Not any that I'm aware of." He cleared his throat with a cough. "As far as I know, the man just arrived from Saint Louis."

Snickering, Jerome shook his head. "Well if he's from Saint Louis, then we probably should trust him. Right, Rondal? Probably everyone in town could vouch for the man."

His brother lifted his torch so it cast its light over the marshal. "That'll be enough, Jerome," the man said. "This is the man that found Zeke so that he did not have to lay out in the rain and mud all night."

Jerome swallowed. "You're right. Sorry, Marshal."

None of them spoke for a while, just listening to the wind and water dripping from the trees. The lantern shone on the path, glinting off the water that streamed down the hill and pooled at its base.

"Well?" Jerome asked. "Do we continue on up?"

The marshal nodded once and nudged his horse in the flank. "Nowhere else to go."

Jerome followed the marshal up the path, and Rondal fell in behind him. Before the marshal's horse even reached the large puddle at the base of the hill, a shot rang out and Jerome heard it whistle above his head. He jerked his horse behind a bush next to the path and jumped out of the saddle. The torch fizzled out when he dropped it. He drew his revolver and pulled the hammer back.

His brother and Marshal Baker hid behind a couple of oaks on the other side of the path. Both had their pistols drawn and cocked, keeping careful to stay behind the trunks. The marshal's hat had fallen off, and the man looked up into the branches above him.

"You don't want to do this, Abner Scott." His gravelly voice seemed to fall flat in the water-logged forest. "Let's talk this out."

From the crest of the hill, Abner snorted. "Is that the Willis boys you got there with you, Marshal?"

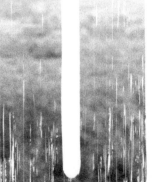

When the man did not get an answer, he shouted even louder. "Then if the Willis boys are there with you, it doesn't seem like you truly want to do a lot of talking, Marshal. I think I'll just take my chances up here."

"Don't be a damn fool, Abner." The marshal shifted his back against the tree and dug his heels into the soft dirt. "I can send someone back to town for a whole mob of men that ain't too happy with you right now. Let's talk this out."

Abner ignored the marshal. "How long will you pursue this vendetta, Jerome?"

"As long as it takes to bring you to justice for killing my father and brother, Abner." Jerome stood and fired three shots up toward the top of the hill. "As long as it takes." He dropped back down behind the bush, one hand holding his pistol and the other gripping the reins to his horse.

The wind picked up and rushed through the treetops. Water, disturbed by the wind, fell like a dumped bucket on top of them.

"Let it go, Jerome." Abner's voice drifted down from somewhere in the dark above. It didn't echo, only settling to the ground like the dampness.

Jerome shook his head and clenched his jaw tight enough he could feel his teeth grinding against each other. His heart raced, and the muscles across his chest tightened enough that it hurt to take a deep breath.

"I will have justice, Abner."

"No you won't." The man's voice sounded steady and firm. "You're not interested in justice. Only revenge."

"What's the difference?" Jerome's own shout echoed in his ears, and he knew he sounded like some raving lunatic. Times like these is when he wished he had just a little of Rondal's patient calmness.

"Let it go, Jerome." Abner's voice sounded like it hadn't moved from the first time. "Let it go, or it will devour you heart and soul from the inside like the consumption. You will be spitting up your own innards."

Across the path, Rondal knelt close to the ground and peered out from behind his tree. He must have dropped his own torch, but he kept his eyes away from the lantern and focused on the shadows above them. With careful, deliberate steps he moved out from behind the tree and crept forward, never looking back in the light and being meticulous enough not to get caught in the glow.

"We're here with the Marshal to bring you in, Abner." His gaze searched the dark, darting every now and then to his brother before returning to the forest. He brushed the water out of his mustache and shifted from one knee to the other to relieve the dull ache in his thighs.

Laughter danced through the trees, and the sound started his heart pumping even faster. The man who found such mirth in the situation had killed their father—he may not have pulled the trigger, but he sure as rain set everything in motion to lead to that one outcome—and had plunged a knife between their brother's ribs. While looking down on Zeke's body, once so full of life, full of piss and vinegar, Jerome remembered thinking that he would never have a chance to get annoyed at him again. He wouldn't hear their mother's exasperated but amused gasps after Zeke would sneak up behind her in the kitchen, goosing her ribs and running around the table to keep her from snapping a dish rag against him. Even Zeke's constant arguing and refusal to see sense would be missed.

"Keep laughing, Abner," Jerome shouted at the top of the hill but kept hunting the gloom for any movement. "You won't find it so funny when you're standing in front of the judge."

"What judge, Jerome?" Another bullet struck the tree Marshal Baker hid behind as he carefully shone his lantern up the hill. "Are you getting all lawyerly like our friend the marshal? Or are you getting all churchy like your mother, boy? I didn't take you for a religious man. I've seen you throw back the whiskey with the best of 'em."

Jerome snorted and dug his boot toe into the muddy ground, ready to spring up the moment he saw something. "Take your pick, Abner. It's not going to matter one bit. You'll be standing in front of one of them."

"Come on, Abner," the marshal said. "Don't make me send back to town for a tracker. You know you're not getting away after this rain."

Rondal had moved up the hill alongside the path about twenty yards above Jerome. The darkness nearly swallowed him up completely, but Jerome could make out his shape whenever he moved every few moments. He lowered back down to the ground and reloaded his revolver with fresh shells, hoping he'd be able to find his brother amongst the shadows again after he finished.

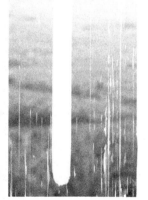

"Come on, Marshal. You're taking their word against mine."

"Are you saying you didn't kill Zeke?" The marshal swept his lantern's beam back and forth through the forest as far up the hill as its light would reach. Jerome cocked the hammer back on his revolver and looked over the top of the bush.

"Not at all, Marshal. The boy attacked me. I was defending myself."

"Then why did you and Luke clear out of town so quick?"

It took Jerome longer than he expected, but he spotted one darker shadow creeping up beside the trail a little further up the hill than when he had last seen Rondal. His hunched form blended in with the night, and Jerome only caught sight of him when he moved. He hoped the marshal would keep the light off the point beside the trail where a couple of large boulders twenty yards further up the slope would force Rondal to take the trail or head deeper into the forest.

"Because I knew this would happen. Those hot-headed Willis boys are not at all level-minded like their father was. Zeke had me at gunpoint, Charles. Anyone tell you that?"

"Then let's head back to town and clear this up."

"Not with Jerome and Rondal down there. My chances of even getting to a fair trial would be next to nothing if that happened."

The wind sighed through the branches, and the light from the lantern flickered a couple of times before flaring back to life as bright as before. Jerome grimaced when his left thigh cramped, and he shifted his weight enough to straighten the leg out to his side.

"Why didn't you mention Luke? He not with you anymore?"

Jerome blinked. The marshal was right. Had the gunslinger slipped away in the shadows?

"He slipped off the back side, Marshal. Crazy one, my sister's kid. Always been a bit touched."

Impossible. Jerome knew the hill. Brambles and loose gravel covered the steep northern face thick enough that not even the wildest horse could be forced into it as it sloped down into Brush Creek. And the only way down the rest of the rock-littered hill was the path in front of them.

"I can't vouch for his safety if he's out here sneaking around in the dark."

"You don't have to, Marshal. He didn't want to wait around and left before Ezra's bloodthirsty boys got here."

The night air had cooled, especially from the heat that had pressed down on them during the funeral, and the dampness seeped through his clothes enough that Jerome shivered. This waiting wore away at his patience. He squinted, searching the hillside for Rondal. Thirty yards up the rise and about five from the path a shadow surged and then halted.

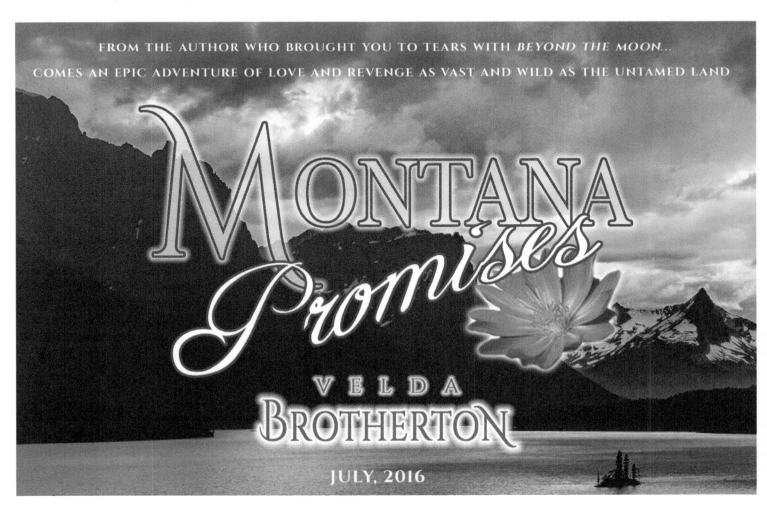

The marshal and Abner continued their back and forth banter, but Jerome focused on his brother's trek up the hillside so that their words became jumbled together. Sounds filled the air in between shouts—water-logged leaves dropping their loads onto the forest floor and some tree frogs that had decided to brave the weather and began tentative start-stop songs. A rock tumbled down the hill to the left of the path, and he thought for a moment that Rondal had slipped. But the sound came from further off the path than his last point.

Light flashed across several tree trunks as the marshal swept his lantern around for the noise. Jerome caught a shadow move ahead of the light, darting behind a broad oak. He leapt around the bush, and keeping the barrel of his gun ahead of him, he raced up the path. The beam moved past the tree, bringing a curtain of thick darkness back down over the forest.

"Bring the light back." Jerome's shout felt thick in his throat. He hoped the marshal had heard him.

The lantern whipped back. One part of the shadow thinned out, reaching towards his brother.

"Move, Rondal."

Jerome lifted the barrel of his gun. A flash of fire leapt out from behind the tree where he had seen the shadow. He pulled the trigger, the Colt bucking in his hand. The lantern lit up the tree, and the shadow pulled away and moved up the hill. He pulled the hammer back again.

The dark shape shifted across the face of the slope and turned back toward him. Jerome squeezed the trigger. The revolver kicked, and the flame lit up the nearby forest. There was a grunt ahead of him. Something heavy fell into the brush and remained still.

With his lantern held aloft, the marshal climbed up the rise and soon stood beside him, shining the light down at the ground. Sightless eyes stared back at them. His second shot had torn through Luke's neck, and scratches across the man's face meant the first shot had struck the tree he had been hiding behind.

Jerome felt his vision sway like something heavy had hit him in the head. His throat constricted, convulsing as if he was about to lose the stew he had eaten several hours ago. He looked around when Rondal came up behind him and put a hand on his shoulder.

"Jerome." Rondal's voice was little more than a whisper.

He turned and looked at his brother. Marshal Baker lifted the lantern, and Rondal's skin was pale and sweat beaded across his forehead.

"Jerome," he said again.

He collapsed to the ground, crumbling like a limp scarecrow taken down from its perch. Jerome went to one knee

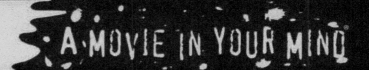

beside his brother, searching for a wound when the marshal shone the light on him.

"There." Marshal Baker pointed to Rondal's right side. "His shoulder. We better pack it and get him back into town. This can wait."

Jerome nodded, agreeing. "Help me get him down to his horse." After he plugged the wound and tightened a strap around his shoulder, the two men carried Rondal.

They rode back into town, barely managing to hold him upright in his saddle between them as they rode through the deserted and darkened streets. It took a few minutes of pounding on the doctor's front door to get the man to open it and let them into the examination room. When they laid him on the table, Rondal grunted but never opened his eyes. The bandage they had wrapped around his shoulder had already soaked through. Jerome sucked air in through his teeth when the doctor shined his lantern on the wound.

The dark outside had shifted to the gray light of early dawn by the time the doctor came out into the front sitting room. Jerome nudged the marshal with his boot, and the man snorted, blinking his eyes rapidly until he could focus.

"He going to be all right?" Jerome pushed himself up out of the straight-backed chair next to the cold fireplace.

Nodding, the doctor looked back and forth between the marshal and Jerome. "Yes. But he is going to need a considerable amount of time to rest and heal."

"Thank you, doctor." Jerome put his hat on and walked to the front door. "I better get home and tell Mama. She's probably hitching the wagon herself right now to come find out where we've been."

Marshal Baker rubbed his eyes with the backs of his forefingers and then nodded, exhaling loudly. "You better. I'll let you know of any changes."

"Yep." He pulled the door open. "And let me know if you form a posse to go get Abner."

The other man clapped him on the shoulder. "Just you worry about your mother right now."

Jerome never looked back after he turned his horse around and heeled it up to an easy trot. Puddles dotted the road as he left the town, and he could hear the dull roar of the swollen Spring River on the east edge of town. The sun suddenly broke through the clouds and bathed the tops of the trees in gold.

• • •

Jerome kicked out with his foot, striking the fence post with his toe. A cow lurched away at the sudden sound, but then returned to worrying at a tuft of grass. Pain lanced up his legs, and he winced. But it didn't hurt enough to take his mind from the betrayal he felt. The rain from the day before had left the air thick and damp with moisture, and the late-morning sun had already heated up the air enough that sweat trickled down his spin and the side of his face.

The high temperature became a problem when combined with the high humidity, keeping the sweat from evaporating and making him feel like he had been covered by a thick blanket in the sun.

"What do you mean you let him go to his house, Marshal?" Jerome snarled the corner of his lip. His hands trembled, and he clenched and relaxed his fingers several times.

He tried to remember that Rondal was resting at the doctor's and Mama already had enough to worry about without dealing with him getting in trouble for beating the marshal. His breath came in deep draws through his nose, filling his lungs like a blacksmith's bellows. The intensity of his anger sent uncomfortable warmth creeping up his chest.

"He should be sitting in a cell at the jailhouse right now, and you know it as well as anyone in this town." Jerome pulled his hat off and wiped the sweat from his brow with the back of his arm. "He didn't buy you, too, did he?"

"Now just a minute." Marshal Baker pointed his finger at him and rested his right hand on the butt of his revolver. "You better not be accusing me of any impropriety."

Jerome shrugged and put his hat back on. "Just seems funny that you would let the man who shot at us last night go without at least putting him in front of a judge."

"He said Luke did all the shooting."

"And you believed him?"

The marshal shook his head. "What I think doesn't come into it. I can't arrest him for something I can't prove in absence of any evidence to the contrary."

Snorting, Jerome leaned against the top rail of the fence and looked out in the field packed with cows that had just been brought up from Texas a couple of nights ago. He lifted his aching foot and rested it on the bottom rail.

"I don't understand that. You and I both know he did it. Let's just round up some men and go get him. We'll wait for your damn trial before we hang him."

Baker sighed, his shoulders slumping as he also leaned against the fence. "Nothing we think is going to influence Judge Horton to convict him without evidence. We still need that confession Zeke was trying to force out of him." He glanced over at Jerome. "How'd your mama take it this morning?"

"Not good." Jerome lowered his head and chewed on his top lip. "I didn't tell her about Rondal yet."

A white cow with a brown splash over its back and neck slurped noisily at a puddle. Jerome watched as it swished its tail lazily, flipping at the flies that hovered around it. Another cow with russet fur walked up beside the other and put its muzzle down into the water beside it, drinking just as loud.

"Do you think old man John Baxter knew this town was going to get so big so quick when he built his trading post?"

"I don't know that I've ever thought about it." Jerome frowned and brushed at a fly that tried to land on his face.

Marshal Baker nodded. "I guess not." He lifted his right hand and pointed out over the field to a broad walnut tree.

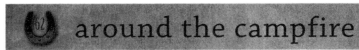

"This land wasn't ready for all these people when they all started showing up."

"You gonna give me a history lesson, Marshal?" Jerome spit between his teeth and watched it arc over the fence out into the field.

"Sounds like I might need to just to keep you from running off faster than your head can keep up."

Jerome scowled, the corners of his mouth tightening. He shook his head and pushed himself off the fence. Before he could turn around, the marshal growled at him.

"Hold on, Jerome." He put a hand on his shoulder. "I want you to take a moment and look out there."

His shoulders drooped, and he let out a long breath of air. "What is it?" After walking back to the fence, he propped his elbows on the fence and blinked a few times.

"Like I was saying," the marshal said, "this land wasn't ready for us when John Baxter came in and built his little trading post. No one knows if he saw something coming that others didn't at the time. Or maybe he just got lucky."

"Okay. But what's this got to do with getting Abner?"

Marshal Baker nodded. "It took a lot of strong men and many of their wives to make this town into what it is today. And your father was one of them."

He waved his hands over the field like he had scattered seeds. "They didn't look at the hardship and turn around. No. They rolled up their sleeves and got to work clearing fields like this one. They built this town up here on the west bank of the Spring River away from the flood plains."

"Come on, Marshal." Jerome rubbed the bridge of nose between his fingers. "I need to check on Rondal and see if Mama's doing all right."

"The point I'm trying to make is that this town didn't build itself in one day." He clapped his hands down against the fence railing. "It took them years of patience and constant work to build it into what we see today."

"I know all this."

The man nodded his head, the corners of his lips curling up in a smirk. "Old news, I know. But those men and women that built this town had patience. You need to have some as well. Our town was built by people with patience who took their time and did it right. We need to do the same with building a case against Abner."

He put his left hand on Jerome's shoulder, giving it a squeeze between his rough fingers. "Let's get this done right. I have no doubt myself that he killed your brother and took those shots at us last night. But if we rush through this, we're not going to like how it ends up."

The two remained silent, watching the cows meander through the field, grazing and drinking from the rain puddles. A crow called out from the top branches of the walnut, and Jerome watched a rabbit sprint into the field before stopping and hopping slowly from one tuft of grass to the other. He wished he had his rifle because rabbit sounded good for supper tonight.

"Okay, Marshall," he said, shrugging the man's hand away. "I'll wait. But I'm just afraid that Abner has already packed up and left town. I don't think he's gonna just wait around for you to arrest him."

Marshal Baker shook his head back and forth. "He gave me his assurances that he would remain in town. He knows I have some questions for him."

"All right. I'd wager against you, but you know Mama frowns on such things."

The other man reached out. "I'll get this done. Don't worry."

Jerome took the offered hand and shook it firmly.

"You do that." He stepped back from the fence and turned around. "I've got to go check on Rondal. You be sure to let me know what happens, will you?"

"I will." Baker nodded once. "I certainly will."

By the time he returned from seeing Rondal, the sun had begun its long crawl below the western horizon. Florence Eaton had stayed the night with mama, and her son-in-low Herschel had come over in the morning to help around the house. When he returned home, he put the saddle and equipment away before taking the time to brush his horse down good. He was only trying to prolong the inevitable—telling Mama that her youngest son's murderer had been let go and that her second son would not be home for supper because he had taken a bullet in the shoulder.

Parson Watkins had come back with him earlier that morning to tell Mama about Zeke, but he couldn't bring himself to explain what had happened to Rondal. Considering that they had just buried her husband, she had not broken into hysterics and wailing as he had expected. Tears had flown freely from her eyes after she had closed them and had dropped to her knees. Missus Eaton had come over and held Mama's trembling hands.

Now he planned to go in and tell her more bad news. He had promised justice, and now they had nothing to show for it. Abner, he was certain, would bolt at the earliest opportunity. The man was probably already hightailing it west, trying to get beyond Marshal Baker's reach.

He stood with one boot on the porch and the other planted firmly on the ground. An orange glow flared through the side window as someone inside lit a lantern. Mumbled voices and an occasional nervous chuckle reached him through the door, but he kept his head down and tried to breathe evenly in long deep breaths through his nose as he had seen Rondal do so many times. It seemed to work for his brother. Why wouldn't it settle his own heart that beat like a caged animal inside his chest? Why was it that everything he tried to do to make things better only made them worse?

With one last quick gasp of air followed by a nervous cough, he walked across the porch and pushed open the front door. Mama sat at the table. She held a steaming cup in her hands but didn't drink as she stared at it. Her head slowly turned when he closed the door behind him. He met her eyes—bloodshot and tired—and immediately rushed to her, tossing his hat onto the table.

He knelt beside her on the floor and rested his head upon her lap. "I'm so sorry, Mama. I can't seem to make anything right. I've let you and Pop down."

She brushed her hand through his hair. "Ssh, Jerome." Her voice sounded calm and even. She didn't sound as tired as she had looked. "It's in God's hands now. Let Him take care of it."

Jerome cleared his throat and swallowed. "I've tried, Mama, but I just can't do it." A tear leaked from the corner of eye just to be soaked up by her apron. "I think He wants me to right this wrong. But I don't know how. Everything I touch goes to hell."

"No, Jerome." Her voice took on the stern edge that had always been present when they were growing up. Mama brooked no argument at times like this. "It's not yours to own. Vengeance is mine, says the Lord. Who are we to thwart His will?"

Still on his knees, he looked up at her and tried to smile. But it stuck on his lips, and he managed nothing more than a grimace. How many times had she sat in this house and try to teach them from the Word? How many times did he and his brothers turn right around and disregard everything she tried to demonstrate to them? How many times was he going to let her down?

"I know what you want me to do, Mama." He grabbed her hands and held them in his own. "But I have to try to set this right."

She nodded and looked beyond him to the door. "Where's Rondal? Is he going to be here for supper?"

"I'm sorry." He squeezed her hands. For a brief moment, the corners of her eyes tightened and her brow creased.

"The marshal and us had Abner and his nephew trapped up near Brush Creek." She pulled her hands free and covered her mouth. He shook his head. "It's all right. Luke tried to sneak up on us, but we got him. Rondal took a bullet in the shoulder."

Mama gasped, and her shoulders started to shake. Missus Eaton put a pan back on the stove and walked over to the table. She put her arms around his mother and looked up at him with a raised eyebrow.

"It's okay." He cupped his hands around her elbows. "The doctor says he should heal right fine without any trouble. It was a clean wound. No shrapnel or debris. There shouldn't be any infection if he keeps it clean."

She nodded slowly. Her breathing eased into long, slow inhales and loud exhales. "But you're going back out there."

Jerome nodded. "I have to, Mama."

"You haven't learned a thing I've taught you, have you?"

He narrowed his eyes as they blurred. "I'm trying, Mama. I just have to do this."

Missus Eaton shook her head back and forth slowly, and she stared at him, not moving her gaze one bit to the left or right.

"Are you doing this for them, Jerome?"

"What do you mean, Missus Eaton?"

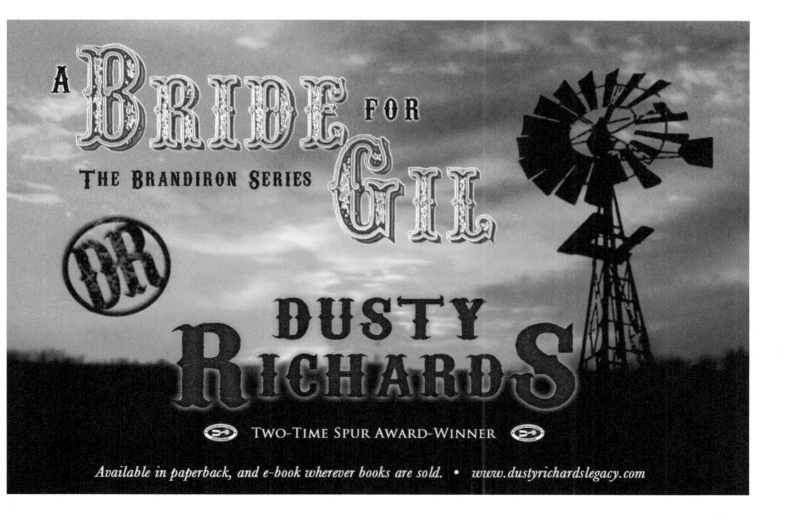

She jabbed a finger at him. "Or are you doing this for you?" She put her hand back down. "Your mother has already lost a husband and a son, with another one hurt to all this trouble. She shouldn't have to worry about something happening to you too. Think about her."

Standing up slowly, he nodded and blew out a long breath through puffed up cheeks. "I am, Missus Eaton." He lowered his head until his mother met his stare. "You may not see this now, Mama, and I know it's hard. But I am doing this for the family. If Abner has fled, like I told the marshal he would, then I will help hunt him down and bring him back for a trial."

His mother grimaced and nodded. She reached out and put her hand on the side of his arm. "Come back whole. We need you whole."

He tried to smile and reassure her, but it probably looked more like a frown. "I will, Mama. I love you."

He turned and walked out the door without looking back. As soon as he stepped off the porch, he realized that he had never intended to do anything but what he was going to do— go after Abner. He should have kept the horse saddled and ready. Now it would be even longer before he made it back into town and start the hunt. He would bring the man to justice no matter how long it took.

• • •

Abner had left a single candle burning on table next to the bed, its flame flickering in the gentle movement of the air as Jerome stepped over to the chair. He let his eyes adjust to the dark, the pupils dilating to let in more light. The chair creaked when he settled into it, enough to cause the sleeping man to snort and roll over to his side. Jerome waited, listening to the sounds outside the single window. If he strained, he could hear the laughter and raucous noise from the Rowdy Joe and their Running of the Doves as naked saloon girls raced from the West bank of the river back to the tavern. He wondered which cowboy won the betting and left with the prize. None of the rowdiness in Baxter Springs prepared him for the lawlessness and lewd atmosphere he found in Delano, Kansas in 1873.

He leaned over and moved Abner's gun belt away, careful not to let it hit against the side of the bed. The man rolled over to his other side and flipped the blanket down off his shoulders. Jerome struck a parlor match and set the flame to the wick in the lantern on the dresser beside him. He closed the lantern window as the glow drove the darkness into the corners of the room.

Abner snorted and jerked awake, reaching around blindly for his gun belt, squinting against the light. He sat up in bed, blinking at Jerome. His eyes darted between the cocked revolver on Jerome's lap and his eyes.

"It's been almost a year, hasn't it, Abner?" He picked up his revolver and put his left leg on top of his right. "Got to say though, I did not think to find you in Delano."

Jerome narrowed his eyes and shook his head when Abner opened his mouth to speak. "But then I realized you wanted to be as far from the law as possible. Since Delano has no law enforcement agency and you won't be far from the cattle shipping business, what better place than right here in the thick of it?"

"What do you want, Jerome?" Abner rubbed at his eyes with the butt of his hands. "Are you still looking for vengeance?"

"No, Abner." He let his thumb rest on the cocked hammer. "I told Mama I would bring you back to stand trial."

"Hmph." Abner grunted and pushed himself further up in the bed. "What's that going to prove?"

Jerome shrugged. "Don't rightly know. But I guarantee I will be at your hanging with a basket lunch. Maybe I'll even hire one of those brass bands to play something festive."

Abner swallowed. His eyes kept lowering to the gun. "What do you want? I've been in this situation before with one of you Willis boys."

Gritting his teeth, his jaw clenching and the fingers of his left hand digging into his palm, Jerome took several deep breaths, trying to calm the racing of his heart. He shook his head, trying to push the image of Zeke's body in the Marshal's office from his mind.

"Why did you do it, Abner? We had a good business partnership."

"How stupid are you boys?" Abner curled his lip back. "How many times do I have to tell you it was Luke that pulled the trigger?"

Jerome shrugged. "What did you want? Why were you at my father's office that night?"

Closing his eyes and leaning over to scratch the back of his neck, Abner said, "Your father was behind the times, boy. He couldn't see the future for it slapping him square in the face." The man opened his eyes and gazed at Jerome. "If we didn't sell that land to the railroad, we'd all have lost money when the iron horses get to Texas."

"I doubt Pop wasn't aware of that."

Abner waved one hand around in the air but kept the other one on his lap. "I can see the future, boy."

"What?" Jerome chuckled. "Are you a magician full of parlor tricks and disappearing rabbits?"

The man motioned out the window. "These Kansas cowtowns are going to fade. The bulk of business has already left Baxter Springs and moved here to Delano and Wichita. Another year or two and it'll be shifted over to Dodge city or maybe even bypass it all together."

Jerome pushed his bottom lip out and shook his head. He leaned over and squinted his left eye so he could look down the barrel of the gun at Abner. "So you knew better than everyone?"

Abner nodded, a smile starting to turn the corners of his mouth up. "Both our families could have been very rich. But your father was a fool."

"Be careful, old man." Jerome extended his hand to point the gun straight at him. "I'm taking you back to Marshal Baker."

"You can still get out of Baxter Springs with some pretty

coin if you act fast." Abner wrinkled his nose and scratched at his nostrils. "But you can't wait."

Jerome kicked his foot off his lap and stood up, keeping the barrel aimed at Abner. "Will that bring my father back, you son-of-a-bitch?" He kicked the man's pants over closer to him. "Now get dressed. We're gonna take a little trip." A wide smile split his face, and he chuckled. "Don't worry about your boots. I'd hate for you to think you had an opportunity to get away. Being bare-foot will slow you down and make you walk more careful."

Shrugging, Abner slid to the side of the bed and tugged his pants on. He nodded at the gun. "You going to keep that on me the whole time, boy? You're going to have to sleep some time."

"I'll manage just fine." He switched the gun from his right hand to his left. "I'll just hog-tie you each night."

The other man pursed his lips and cocked his right eyebrow. "You might be as stupid as your little brother, you know that." He stepped closer to Jerome until the barrel of the gun pressed against his chest. "Zeke thought he could bring me in and force a confession out of me. What do you think you can do different?"

Jerome clenched his jaw and exhaled through his nose. He pressed the revolver into the man's chest with his left hand and reached into his right pocket with the other. His hand gripped the pommel of the knife they had found in the water-logged alley behind the Silverlight saloon.

Without a warning, Abner twisted at the waist. His hands flew across his body faster than Jerome could see and sent the Colt flying from his hands. As Abner turned back around and jumped straight at him, Jerome pulled the knife free and jammed the blade into the left side of Abner's chest.

The man grunted, and then staggered back onto the bed. He held his hand against the wound, but blood, black in the dim light, seeped through his fingers and spread across his nightshirt. Looking at Jerome, he swallowed. His lips pulled back from his teeth, and he blinked as if he couldn't keep his eyes open.

Jerome walked to the edge of the bed and looked down at the man. Abner's face paled, and he started to shiver. The blood leaked from his wound and stretched onto the bed beneath him. He glared at Jerome, his lips moving as he groaned as if searching for something to say but not finding the words.

Stepping closer, Jerome leaned over the bed until his lips were beside the man's ear. "Not so stupid after all, I guess. I thought you might want this back."

He stood up and watched as Abner's blinking grew faster and more erratic, his eyes opening and closing without any pattern. His breath came in shorter and quicker gasps until he let out a long exhale and stopped blinking.

Jerome pulled the knife from the man's chest and set it on the dresser. He cupped his hand over the lantern chimney and blew,

sending the room back into darkness except for the tiny candle flame that flickered a couple more times before it too went out.

He walked over to the door and put his hand on the handle. Glancing back at the shadow lying atop the bed, he sniffed once.

"I'm sorry, Mama."

He walked out of the room and shut the door.

* * *

Jerome sat on his porch in Americana, Brazil, sweat beading up on his forehead and running down his temple. The heat and humidity here were both worse than they had been in southeast Kansas, but at least here he was far from curious neighbors and inquisitive officials. Here he supplied goods and equipment to the new cotton plantations that had sprung up across the country after the end of the American Civil War and Emperor Dom Pedro II had encouraged emigration.

During the war, he had fought briefly with the North in a Kansas regiment, but he remained silent about his political opinion in Brazil. Each morning he woke and drove his wagon to the market and sold his services out to anyone that needed to deliver orders to outlying plantations. And he kept his head down in order to not attract any unwanted attention.

He glanced at the letter in his hand, reading it once more.

Dearest Brother Rondal,

I have found steady work and am able to support myself and even keep a little back to invest in other endeavors to help this place prosper. I will burden neither you nor Mama with my location so that you will not be bothered by others.

Know that I am sorry that I failed our family. I let Pop and Zeke down most of all. How I wish that I had your temperament. It would have come in handy during all those mistakes I made. If only I had thought before I acted.

I thought it was in the best interest of the family, but I realize now that it was the best thing to appease my own inner turmoil. Please, accept my apology for all I have done.

Please tell Mama that I am sorry and that I love her.

Your loving and loyal brother,
Jerome Michael Willis.

He carefully folded up the letter and sealed it in an envelope. In the morning, on the way to pick up his next load, he would send it. The evenings were always hot, but not to the sweltering extent that they were deeper inland farther away from the ocean. A breeze came up and ruffled his hair. A thin sheen of sweat covered his ever-darkening skin.

Some strange bird or animal called out from the forest. He wondered if he would ever get used to the changes in his world.

JC Crumpton

Some are born with a silver spoon, but award-winning author JC Crumpton came out of the womb with a pen and a notebook. A cancer survivor, when not writing, reading or working as an analyst, he will often be on the trails or in the gym training for an ultra-marathon or powerlifting—complete with grunts and screams in appropriate places—or volunteering for various charities.

JC received his undergraduate degree in English with a Creative Writing Emphasis from the University of Arkansas and worked seven years for a daily newspaper, compiling a list of over 1,000 bylines.

Field of Strong Men is JC's first Western. More of his work has appeared in *Aiofe's Kiss, Beyond Centauri,* and *The Penwood Review,* among others. He has several projects coming out with Pro Se Press and Oghma Creative Media, including his first novel, *Silence in the Garden,* which is set to hit bookshelves in early 2017. He is a proud member of Authors' Anonymous writing group, the Northwest Arkansas Writers' Workshop, Ozarks Writers' League, and Ozark Creative Writers.

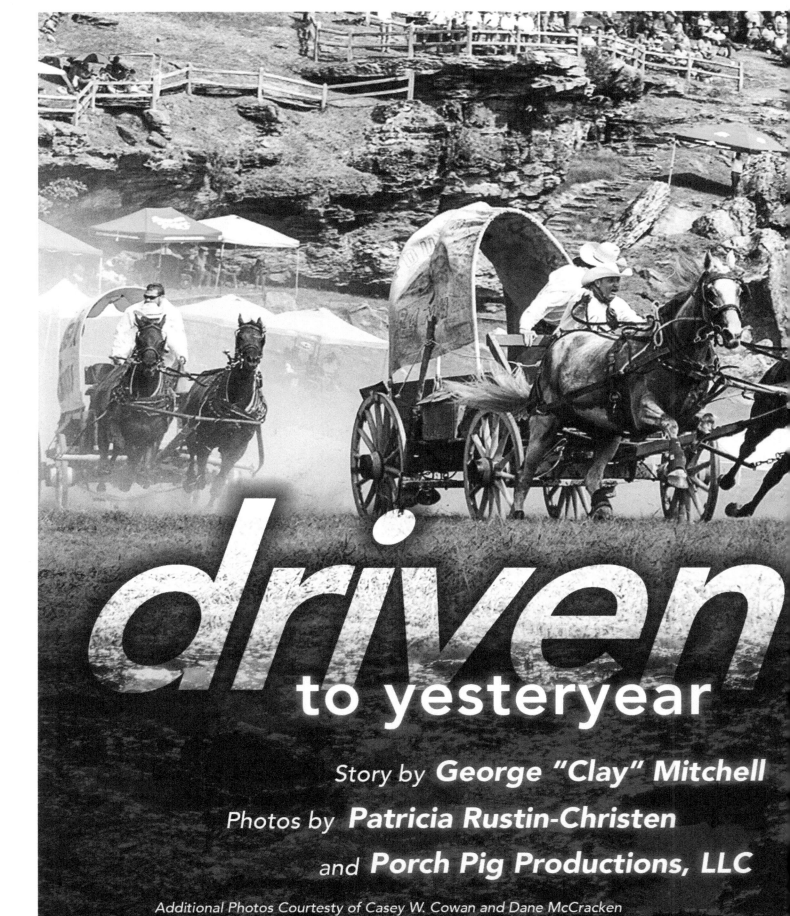

driven
to yesteryear

Story by **George "Clay" Mitchell**

Photos by **Patricia Rustin-Christen**
and **Porch Pig Productions, LLC**

Additional Photos Courtesty of Casey W. Cowan and Dane McCracken

one family's

passion

fuels America's

largest

equestrian sporting event

ōf ranch

For Dan and Peggy Eoff at the Bar ōF Ranch hosting the annual Chuckwagon Races around Labor Day Weekend in Clinton, Ark., has become a part of who they are and what they do.

"I can't put my finger on it, but I'm still shocked the chuckwagon races are still an interest," said Peggy from her Western Store, also located on the ranch. "We had people coming since the first one. They tell us 'this is our vacation every year and we wouldn't miss it.' They must have a good time. They get beautiful scenery and a chance to play cowboy."

It's the chance to play cowboy that makes the annual Labor Day event a unique experience. While the races have continued

and barrel racing. So, it's not just a sit-and-watch event. They can be part of what's going on and not just a spectator."

Peggy said folks yearn for the opportunity to get out into nature and be a cowboy, to get back to a "simpler time when things aren't so crazy out there."

"People are always seem fascinated in doing what is right and being independent... doggone it, that just might be it," said Peggy. "There was a time you could ride where you wanted to and not have anybody right next to you. Now, so many people live in town and may not have the opportunity to ride alongside a river or over a mountain. We try to provide that for them."

The event begins on Saturday, Aug. 27 and lasts until Sept. 4 with participants of all ages.

"We had a lady come into the store to let us know her grandson will be running the wagon. She'll still be in the back, but she'll let him have the reins," said Peggy. "There are some who were here as a baby, but are now racing."

The beginning of the chuckwagon races started nearly 30 years ago.

The Eoffs would visit friends during the holidays and wanted to do something at their home for Labor Day. Their original house at the time was only 700 sq. ft. On one vacation, the Eoffs went with some friends to the Frontier Day Rodeo held in Cheyenne, Wyoming, where they witnessed a chuckwagon race.

> **"They tell us 'this is our vacation every year and we wouldn't miss it.' They must have a good time. They get beautiful scenery and a chance to play cowboy."**

to grow, other activities soon became part of the event.

"At first, we thought people would just come to watch, but some wanted to participate," Peggy said. "We added trail rides and little competitions. We have a camper's rodeo with roping

the ranch

"It was our turn to do our part and Dan isn't one to just sit around and visit," said Peggy. "He wanted to do a wagon race and at night have a potluck while everyone talked about what they did that day."

The Eoffs were off and running.

They contacted friends, including local rodeo announcer Danny Newland, who broadcasted at a bull-riding event about the Eoffs hosting a chuckwagon race at the ranch. The Eoffs were expecting about 150 the first year, but 500 spectators showed up to watch the first eight wagons race. Peggy thinks more would have shown up, but the dirt road up the mountain to the ranch may have deterred some.

"The next time Dan was at the coffee shop, everyone was talking about the races. Dan's mind gets spinning, he's an entrepreneur, he thinks if we promoted just a little, make it two days, more people will show," said Peggy

For several weekends leading up to the next big event, the Eoffs traveled around to various country stores and other places to promote the chuckwagon races. They didn't get the thousands they were expecting the next year, but they had 32 competing and the next year had 68.

The Eoffs don't count the people who come out each year to watch the event. Some estimates put between 10,000 and 20,000 folks making the journey to the ranch in Van Buren County.

"We don't count people, we count horses because we have to check their papers," Peggy said. The ranch hosted over 6,000 horses, a peak number, back in 2010, but the numbers have dwindled to 4,800 last year. "We're not sure why it has

there's chuckwagons and there's **chuckwagons**

do you know the difference?

American chuckwagon racing is a little different from its Canadian counterpart.

The American divisions are based on the size and types of animals used in the race (ponies, mules, and horses). An additional division includes the use of the classic wooden wagon pulled by the bigger horses and another which is a straight shot called The Oklahoma Land Rush.

In all divisions, there are three competitors on each team, a driver, a cook and an outrider. Each team begins outside the wagon. At the start, the team has to "break" camp which consists of putting the tent and the "stove" into the back of the wagon and takes off. The outrider races his mount towards the finish line, followed as closley as possible by the wagon. It's a timed competition, but penalties if not all the "equipment" or personnel reaches the finish line, or if the wagon beats the team's horse.

"While nobody wants to see any person or animal hurt, but if there's a wreck you want to be there to see it," said Peggy Eoff, co-organizer of the Chuckwagon Racing National Championship in Clinton, Arkansas. "It's like NASCAR. It'll definitely give you something to talk about."

Aside from the Oklahoma Land Rush division, the rest of the wagons race in a track in the shape of nine. The mule division will have a hill to climb, which differentiates the race from the other divisions.

the races

decreased. The crowd seems steady. We may not be growing, but we're still holding our own."

Dan was born and raised in Clinton and bought the ranch in 1977 and had the first house built in 1980. Peggy and Dan raised both of their children at the ranch. Their daughter, Dapple and son-in-law Dane McCracken work alongside with them with the operations of the ranch and preparation for the chuckwagon races. The Eoffs also have a son, Sky Eoff, who is in the Navy.

"We're roped in, and we can't quit now. This is just who we are and we want to entertain people. We must have some of that Buffalo Bill and Wild West Show blood in us. This is just another way we can live the western life," said Peggy. "For Dan, it has always been about being a cowboy. He would watch the Lone Ranger as a kid and go out to ride his pony. I was raised in the country, but when we got married, it became my way of life."

Peggy said after 30 years they have the prep work down to the day. She knows when May rolls around she starts sending out letters to vendors and begins her checklist of things to do. Dan does his part with taking the fences down, mowing and moving the cattle.

"Our kids grew up in this and (Dapple) works with me side-by-side, and my son-in-law helps Dan. We have three granddaughters to train them up to help as well. For us, this has always been about family."

—*George "Clay" Mitchell is an award-winning reporter and photographer. When he's not on the trail writing for* Saddlebag Dispatches, *he works for the* Crawford County Press-Argus Courier *in Van Buren, Arkansas, where he has served as Sports Editor for many years.*

"There was a time you could ride where you wanted to and not have anybody right next to you. Now, so many people live in town and may not have the opportunity to ride alongside a river or over a mountain. We try to provide that for them."

"It's not just a sit-and-watch event. They can be part of what's going on and not just a spectator."

the people

the boss

Bar ōF Ranch owner and founder Dan Eoff greets the crowd during the opening ceremonies of the 2015 National Championship Chuckwagon Races in Clinton, Arkansas.

trackside proposal

During a break in the action at the East of Mississippi Chuckwagon Races, bronc rider Corey Tackitt goes old school, getting down on bended knee to ask his sweetheart, Elizabeth Cole, for her hand in marriage. Of course, she said, "Yes!"

mule power
hybrid before
hybrids
were cool

a powerful combination

For those unfamiliar with the particulars of mules, a mule is the result of mating a male donkey and a female horse. When a male horse and female donkey reproduce, the resulting offspring is known as a "hinny." While there is a difference, to the layman, mules and hinnys are usually just grouped together under the name 'mule.' Saddle mules are purposely bred from mares with superior riding traits, as such, and are considered better for racing.

Mules are able to carry more weight and have greater stamina than horses because of their hybrid traits. They possess a unique mix of strength and personality, with the sure-footedness, patience and endurance of an ass, but the energy and personality of the horse.

Mules are either run as a 2-by-2 team or 4 abreast, depending upon the choice of the driver. With the 2-by-2 team, only the front two mules are controlled, but the 4 abreast gives the driver control of all the mules at once. The mules are often utilized to race up and down hills because they're steadier on their feet in comparison to horses. Drivers rely upon slapping the drive lines to motivate the mules. Trying to whip a mule into submission is a bad idea—an insult the mule won't easily forget. There's an old saying that if all horses were trained with the patience it takes to train a mule, there would be a lot better horses in the world.

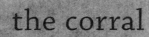

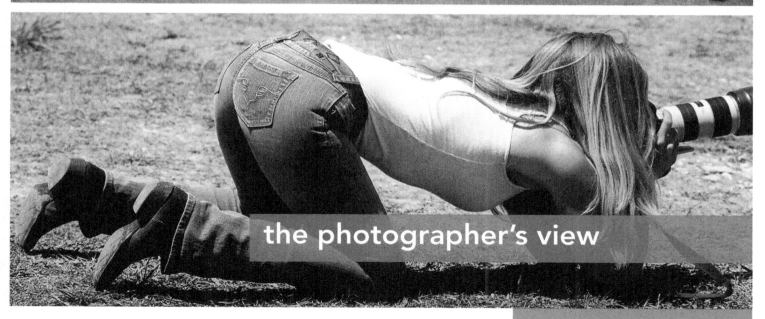

the photographer's view

Dear Racers and fans,

It's a very rare magazine that gives a photographer the opportunity to address their readers and say "thank you" for allowing me to climb all over and under your trailers, putting up with a view of my fanny while I'm bending around trying to get the shot I want, holding my equipment while I jump into rivers, the offers of water when I am melting down and to all the safety personnel at the events I attend for keeping an eye on me. I have to be extreme in order to capture the extreme subjects I photograph and your generosity and good humor allows me to give a 100%.

I am so proud of this article by *Saddlebags Dispatch* for representing the sport of Chuckwagon Racing as a whole and look forward to making them my Chuckwagon Racing home. You will still find me visiting the neighbors with other publications that support the sport of Chuckwagon racing but to see how the whole story unfolds you will want to visit Saddlebags dispatch. When I am away from Chuckwagon racing you will find Porch Pig Productions taking up residence at *Mules and More* Magazine representing some of the finest long eared athletes in the country.

It is important to note that all of the images featured in this article were financially sponsored in whole or part by East of the Mississippi Chuckwagon Races and Reeds Plumbing. Keep making memories.

Prayers of respect and peace to each of you
Patricia Rustin-Christen
Porch Pig Productions

2016 national championship chuckwagon races

schedule of events

saturday, august 27

Gates Open: 8 a.m.
3 & 4 Year-Old Bronc Futurity: 7 p.m. (Arena)
Concert (TBA): 8 p.m. (Bunkhouse)

sunday, august 28

Horse Drive, Cattle Drive: 9 a.m. (Arena)
Cowboy Church: 11 a.m. (Arena)
Cowboy Mounted Shooting: 1 p.m. (Arena)
(guns and ammo provided)
TBA: 8 p.m. (Bunkhouse)

monday, august 29

Bucking Bull Futurity (2 year-old), 6:30 p.m. (Arena)
Calcutta: 7:30 p.m. (Arena)
Bucking Bull Futurity (3 year-old): 9 p.m. (Arena)
Maturity (5 year-old): 9 p.m. (Arena)

Admission: Sat. (Aug 27)–Sat. (Sept. 3): Adults $30 per day.
Sunday, Sept 4th, $20 for Adults, $10 for Children (6-12).
*All clinics, events and competitions have no entry fee

tuesday, august 30

Jackpot Roping: 9 a.m. 2G (Arena)
Team Sorting Clinic: 10 a.m. (Arena)
Trail Ride (Horses & Wagons): 3 p.m. (Bottom Barn)
Fish Fry: 5 p.m. (Clinton Park)
Roping Clinic: 6 p.m. (Arena)
Karaoke: 7 p.m. (Bunkhouse)
Barrel Racing Clinic: 7:30 p.m. (Arena)
TBA: 8 p.m. (Hotel)

wednesday, august 31

Trail Ride Clinic: 9:30 a.m. (Arena)
Trail Ride (Horses & Wagons): 10:30 a.m. (Bottom Barn)
Chuckwagon BBQ: 12 p.m. (Pond)
Horseshoeing Clinic: 3 p.m. (Arena)
Showing of Select Horses & Mules: 4 p.m. (Arena)
Select Horse and Mule Sale: 6 p.m. (Arena)
Chuckwagon Camp Cookoff: 7 p.m. (Bunkhouse)
Lee Greenwood Concert: 8 p.m. (Hotel)

thursday, september 1

Trail Ride & Xtreme Trail Ride: 8:30 (Arena)
(No Wagons Allowed, approx. 4 hour ride)
Working Cow Dog Show: 10 a.m. (Arena)
Rookie Qualifying & Pasture Roping: 1 p.m. (Track)
Mule Clinic: 4 p.m. (Arena)
Team Sorting, Barrel Race: 5 p.m. (Arena)
(Campers & Contestants Only, Register Between 3-4 p.m.)
Used Tack Auction: 6 p.m. (Bunkhouse)
Go-Round Presentations: 7 p.m. (Saloon)
Opening Act (TBA): 7:30 p.m. (Hotel)
Randy Rogers Band Concert: 8 p.m. (Hotel)

friday, september 2

Trail Ride Competition: 9 a.m. (Arena)
Chuckwagon Race (First): 1 p.m. (Track)
Mules Only Competition: 4 p.m. (Arena)
Camper's Ranch Rodeo: 6 p.m. (Arena)
(enter by Aug. 15)
Go-Round Presentations: 6 p.m. (Saloon)
Calcutta: 6:30 p.m. (Saloon)
Opening Act (TBA): 7:30 p.m. (Hotel)
Aaron Tippin Concert: 8 p.m. (Hotel)

saturday, september 3

Preshow & Pasture Roping Finals: 11 a.m. (Track)
Chuckwagon Race (Second): 1 p.m. (Track)
Horse Sale: 5 p.m. (Arena)
Bluegrass Music (TBA): 7 p.m. (Hotel)
Go-Round Presentations: 7 p.m. (Saloon)
Kid's Ranch Rodeo: 8 p.m. (Arena)
Buffalo Rock Dance: 8 p.m. (Hotel)
Tulsa Playboys: 8 p.m. (Hotel)

sunday, september 4

Non-Denominational Church Services: 9 a.m.
(Announcer's Stand)
Cowboy Church: 9 a.m. (Arena)
Preshow: 11 a.m. (Track)
Chuckwagon Race (Final): 1 p.m. (Track)
Awards Ceremony (1 hour after final race) (Saloon)

Events are tentative and may be subject to change. (Visit www. chuckwagonraces.com/2016-race-schedule/ for any changes).

SKY STONE

a short story

John T. Biggs

author of
Sacred Alarm Clock & Cherokee Ice

Bird Singer didn't like anything about peyote, the bitter taste, the way it made the moon twist across the night sky, and especially the nausea. He tried not to think about it while he chewed dried cactus buttons. Waiting was the hardest part of a vision quest; a holy man needed patience.

"Help me." His prayer was weak, but so was his magic. Rain callers could make demands of the spirits, but a shaman like Bird Singer had to beg for visions like a camp dog at the cooking fire.

"Please help me."

Coyotes sang to him from across the desert. Whether that was a good sign or bad remained to be seen. He released a pinch of corn pollen into the air, and grasped the amulet bag he wore around his neck. Most of his helping spirits didn't fly at night, but he called on them anyway. Lives hung in the balance.

A coyote bit a woman three days ago. Would a killing spirit fill her mouth with foam? Would sickness spread through the pueblo? He needed answers.

The wind nudged Bird Singer along a path through stray boulders and jojoba plants, just as she'd done on the day his spirit helper chose him—the proudest day of his life, when he brought the red-backed hawk down from the sky with a single pebble from his sling.

Bird Singer moved where the wind pushed him until he came to a solitary set of Hopi sandal prints. What fool would travel alone at night? His eyes followed the gentle curve of the trail until he found the answer.

I am the fool. Tricked into a circle. Peyote's laughter filled the air, like music from an abalone shell wind chime.

Then the melody stopped, replaced by harsh Apache words and more coyote songs.

Were the marauders and the tricksters laying traps? With spirits, nothing was certain.

"Help me."

A yellow light flashed in the western sky and five red streaks reached toward the world. A dust cloud rose where the nearest bright finger touched the desert. Now Bird Singer knew where Peyote intended him to go, but he was in no hurry.

• • •

The Apache lay face down between a smoldering fire and a blanket. Bird Singer hid in the brush and weighed the possibilities. No breathing motions, but Apaches were famous for deception.

The shaman held his breath until he couldn't hold it any longer. He held it three more times. Even an Apache warrior couldn't go so long without breathing.

Bird Singer moved on all fours, like big cat stalking a rabbit. He knew little about Apaches, but he knew this: the raiders seldom traveled alone, and they never ventured far from camp after sunset. There was only one explanation for this solitary warrior. The dead man was a shaman, like Bird Singer. He'd been seeking supernatural wisdom when the spirits struck him down.

The items on the dead man's blanket confirmed Bird Singer's suspicion—a falcon's wing, a copper bell, and two perfectly round rocks with mineral patterns that made them resemble human eyes. The contents of the holy man's medicine bundle

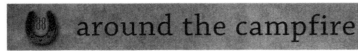

were laid out to attract helping spirits. The fist-size hole in his back was evidence the magic didn't work.

Bird Singer rolled the holy man over so his eyes were open to the sky. He removed an eagle feather from his amulet bag and brushed it first across his own lips, then across the dead man's.

"The sacred lands don't welcome you," he said. "Carry this message to your brothers."

Death's touch had made a hole straight through the Apache, and left a depression in the sand filled to the top with blood.

Like a ceremonial cup, an offering to the living desert. Did it hold anything else? A power object Bird Singer could add to his amulet bag? The Hopi shaman plunged his arm into the warm dark liquid, staining his tunic sleeve to the elbow.

His hand closed on the spirit gift. He lifted it from the pool of blood and rolled in his hand: a lump of shining metal with a surface like a glistening collection of bubbles. Heavier than stone, and warm to the touch.

Peyote whispered, "Spider Woman's gift."

Bird Singer closed his eyes and chanted a prayer for guidance. When he opened them, he saw the silhouettes of three large dogs at the top of a nearby hill. After a dozen heartbeats, an Apache warrior joined the dogs—then another, and another.

One of the warriors shouted a command, and the animals charged.

How did Spider Woman mean for a Hopi holy man stop three war dogs? There had to be a way. The gods didn't bestow gifts on a man one moment and kill him in the next.

The dead man's medicine bundle. The two eye stones on the Apache holy man's blanket were the perfect size for Bird Singer's sling. He loaded one stone at a time and sent them flying.

Two solid cracks, like a cottonwood limb breaking under the weight of ice. Two of the three charging animals fell to the ground with fissures in their skulls large enough to free their souls. The third dog skidded to a stop. He might have run away but the warriors on the hilltop urged him on.

No more eye stones on the blanket. The falcon's wing and copper bell were useless.

The sky stone. Would Spider Woman strike him dead for using it? The dog would surely kill him if he didn't.

"Forgive me!" He loaded the sky stone into his sling and sent it flying. Bird Singer followed the path of the power object in the moonlight. The silver talisman pierced the throat of the charging animal in a gush of blood.

The Apache warriors moved cautiously down the hill. They'd watched him dispatch three battle-hardened dogs with a weapon favored by children.

As they approached, he drew a deep breath and made his owl call. The night birds carried souls to the land of the dead. He hoped Apaches knew it, too. Three more calls in quick succession, then he clutched his amulet bag and waited for the magic.

Four perfect calls brought the Apaches to a stop, but they didn't break and run until a great horned owl flew out of the darkness and perched on the dead man's chest.

Bird Singer ran as well, and while he ran, he sang a song of thanks to Spider Woman.

• • •

"Where is this power object?" Six elders ruled Bird Singer's pueblo. Each one asked him the same question. This time the interrogator was old lady Larkspur, matriarch of the Ant Clan.

"Why didn't Spider Woman give her gift to a rain maker?"

Bird Singer tried to plead his case without sounding argumentative. "The spirits toss. The shaman catches."

Old lady Larkspur wasn't convinced. Bird Singer used a power object to kill a dog, not the stuff of legends.

"What of the coyote?" Five elders already asked that question, but that didn't stop the matriarch from asking it again. "And the woman who was bitten?"

In the end, they believed enough to send scouts looking for Apache raiders. They posted sentries and planned ceremonies.

As old lady Larkspur put it, "The spirits favor those who take precautions."

• • •

Several days passed with no signs of the raiders. There were rumors of Ute warriors attacking a Tewa pueblo twelve days' walk to the north; perhaps Bird Singer had seen stragglers from that battle.

"Or perhaps," one of the elders suggested, "Peyote played a trick on the shaman."

Even Bird Singer began to have his doubts. He'd gone into the desert seeking a coyote vision; perhaps the trickster filled his mind with nonsense.

The shaman purified his body in a sweat lodge, denied himself food and water, and prayed for guidance from the creatures of the air. He sat cross-legged in the plaza focusing his mind on the pristine spirit of the red-backed hawk, when a vulture fluttered from the sky and landed at his side.

Bird Singer opened his eyes and watched the vulture pace around him. "Welcome, Bird Who Cleans The World. What news have you brought me?" The vulture made four circles around the shaman, each one larger than the last. People gathered in the plaza to watch the vulture do what vultures never did.

"The bird has been poisoned!" suggested an old man. It was possible. Alkali salts covered low-lying regions of the desert. Rivulets of water ran through them and collected in poison pools. Perhaps an animal drank from one of these pools, died, and was eaten by this vulture.

"Look!" a young girl shouted, "The bird's foot prints make a power spiral."

The vulture's path formed the familiar twisted pattern the Hopi used to decorate their pots, the same pattern they used to plant corn and beans. No one doubted this vulture was a spirit messenger.

The carrion eater stopped pacing, hopped over to Bird Singer, and regurgitated the contents of its stomach directly in front of him. It made a slow, graceful turn, tested its wings, and ran south, the direction of good news. The Bird Who Cleans the World launched itself into the air and rode the wind over the horizon.

Something silver glittered among clumps of dog fur, deteriorated muscle, and strands of intestine. The shaman reached into the partially digested remains and retrieved the sky stone. He held it up so that everyone around him could see. Now they would have to believe him.

• • •

Discussions of the spirit visitation buzzed in every household. People spoke in whispers whenever the holy man approached. The story of the vulture and the sky stone took on the features of a legend. The problem was, no one knew how the story would end.

No one had seen anything like the sky stone. Its glittering surface exceeded the brightest gloss a skilled artisan could produce on the richest nugget of native copper. Some of the older villagers had seen polished discs of gold carried by traders from the distant south, but even those treasures hadn't sparkled like Spider Woman's gift.

"There is nothing to fear," the shaman promised, but old lady Larkspur told him to keep the talisman out of sight.

"It has killed an Apache holy man and a war dog," she said, "then traveled in the belly of a carrion eater." No one could imagine what kind of power the sky stone held.

"It killed an enemy of the Peaceful People," he told the old woman. "It fell from the heavens. It was lost and then returned by a creature of the sky."

The Shaman placed the sky stone into his amulet bag. At least the people believed in Bird Singer's Apaches, even if the scouts found nothing.

"The spirits took me to the enemy once before," Bird Singer told the elders. "Perhaps they'll do it again."

But the War Chief refused his company. "A man might be in the spirits' favor one moment, and broken out in boils the next. My men won't walk beside a wizard."

The shaman didn't like the sound of that. It was a small step from wizardry to witchcraft. When things went wrong, people went looking for a witch. If the rain failed to come, if the corn failed to grow, if a sickness swept the pueblo, a witch could find himself buried in a shallow grave with a large stone pinning his soul under the earth. When he heard people refer to the Apaches as "the shaman's spirit enemies" he knew it was time to act.

• • •

The night sky was familiar but not friendly. The quarter moon provided barely adequate light, and shooting stars flew across the heavens at a rate of one or two in every hundred heartbeats.

Bird Singer comforted himself with mental chants to keep the forces of world in balance. His life would find its center again once the Apaches were discovered. The coyotes would regain their fear of people. Bird Singer could resume his place as a lesser shaman whose principal function was persuading eagles to give up their feathers.

A cloud of bats fluttered across the moon. The tiny creatures consorted with spirits of the sky after the sun had set, but in the daylight hours they hid in caves. Bats concealed themselves almost as well as Apache raiders.

Could that be a message? Caves were good for hiding bats and Apaches.

Perhaps the night fliers would help a holy man who could speak with owls. Bird Singer removed the sky stone from his amulet bag and held it in his hand. He rolled the sky stone through his fingers, appreciated its complex cobbled surface in the moonlight, offered a prayer of gratitude, then tossed it high into the air.

A large bat dove and caught it.

Chief of the bat tribe.

When bats are fooled into snatching tossed stones, they drop them quickly, but the Bat Chief didn't do this. He carried the sky stone high above his tribe. The talisman glittered in the moonlight like a star, and when the bat released the power object, it fell so slowly that Bird Singer caught it easily in his extended hand.

"Thank you, brother."

The dark flyers made a slow turn in front of the crescent moon. They fluttered across the night sky in a swirling motion easy to follow from the ground. The shaman fell behind, but moonlight glittered on the creatures' wings like sparks carried on a gentle breeze.

By the time he lost sight of his spirit guides, the holy man could hear the voices of Apache warriors. He crouched, still holding the sky stone. The raiders had chosen their cave wisely. Its mouth opened onto an empty part of the sacred land. Cracks in the rock carried smoke from their fire through a thousand tiny chimneys where it wouldn't be seen even in the full light of day.

Twenty warriors sat around a smoldering fire, boasting, laughing, and pulling chunks of meat from a charred leg of venison. Hopi archers could make short work of this lot. Bird Singer held the talisman in his open hand and offered a prayer of thanks.

The Texas-Mexico border, the winter of 1886—The Great Die Up. A raw rift separates Mexicans and Anglos. A loner cowpoke and a mute Mexican girl fight man and nature to reunite against insurmountable odds.

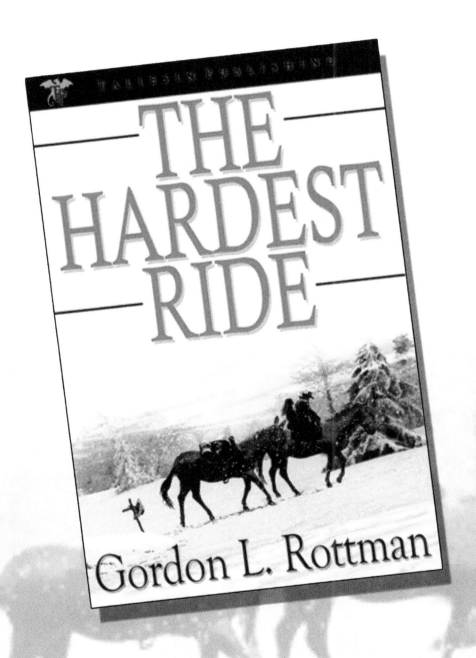

Winner, Western Fictioneers Peacemaker Award for Best Western Novel
Finalist, Western Fictioneers Best First Western Novel
Western Writers of America Spur Award Finalist- Best Traditional Western

http://www.amazon.com/The-Hardest-Ride-Gordon-Rottman-ebook/dp/B00H3U408S
Available from all e-book outlets.
Now also available in trade paperback and audio formats.

The sky stone was a dazzling gift. It concentrated the intensity of ambient light while holding the distorted images of the stars and moon on its cobbled surface. Bird Singer watched the entire night sky roll around his palm. The reflected light pulsed and flashed in cadence with his prayer. The effect pulled at his mind the way trickling water draws a restless spirit into sleep. For a handful of heartbeats he forgot about Apaches.

Then the light dimmed. It had been weeks since the Rain Callers had been about their business and the sky was completely clear. It was not a cloud that obscured the illumination of the stars and moon. The shaman rolled the stone a little more, and a face reflected from its surface, an Apache face.

Without breaking the rhythm of his prayer, Bird Singer found a rock almost too large to hold in his hand. He stood, turned, and threw the stone in a single movement without stopping to aim.

Masau, the god of life and death, was the shaman's ally that night. His rock struck a large Apache warrior squarely in the forehead. The man went down without a sound.

Only one!

Bird Singer felt the warrior's chest, no heartbeat. He heard the Apache's soul escape with his final breath. The shaman looked back into the cave. Two dogs stood in the entrance, taking in his scent. They bared their teeth, put back their ears. It wouldn't take the warriors long to notice.

There were plenty of stones on this mountainside. Bird Singer found two suitable for his sling. In less than ten beats of a frightened heart, the dogs fell dead at the mouth of the cave.

Before the animals stopped twitching, the shaman mimicked the sound of the great horned owl—Four calls, quickly followed by another four. The effect on the raiders was immediate.

Bird Singer recognized a few words: witch, demon, evil spirit. He made four more owl calls, tucked Spider Woman's gift into his amulet bag, then broke into an easy run.

Only after his breath grew ragged did he risk a look behind him. One lone warrior walked toward him from the direction of the cave. One more than he anticipated.

Bird Singer picked up his pace as much as the uneven terrain and the darkness would allow. He expected the warrior to give up the chase and return to the safety of his cave, but the man's silhouette remained a constant feature on the mountain landscape. The warrior plodded across the desert carrying neither bow nor lance. He meant to tear the life away from the Hopi shaman with his bare hands. Or worse, he'd capture Bird Singer, take him to his band's main encampment, and give him to their women.

The sun peeked over the edge of the world as Bird Singer reached his valley. Only half a morning's run to his pueblo if the Apache didn't kill him.

When Bird Singer looked back over his shoulder one last time, the warrior broke into a full sprint, closing the distance between them with every pace.

The shaman clasped his amulet bag and prayed as he ran. Only the spirits could save him. The holy man's heart raced like a sparrow hawk's. His muscles burned enough to double him over. His chest ached. The rush of blood through his ears sounded like the ghosts of his ancestors calling him to the afterlife.

Bird Singer stopped running. He turned to face his death.

The Apache slowed, no longer in a hurry to finish things.

The shaman would either escape or die this day; he would not be taken alive. He opened his amulet bag and removed the sky stone. The talisman had saved him twice before. Perhaps it would save him again.

"Power is with me!" Bird Singer looked to the heavens and chanted, holding the sky stone in the open palm of his left hand. "My need is great."

His adversary stood twenty paces away. He'd drawn an obsidian stiletto and assumed a fighting stance, but his eyes were not turned toward the shaman.

A large male coyote moved from the shadow of a boulder and fixed his attention on the Apache. Foam dripped from the animal's muzzle; it staggered as it moved toward the warrior. If this was the same animal that attacked the woman from Bird Singer's pueblo, evil days lay ahead of her. The bite of such a creature would turn a human into a monster.

No one deserved such a death, not even an Apache marauder.

The warrior stepped backward, matching the coyote pace for pace. He knew the demon would own his body, even if he killed the animal it possessed. He held his stiletto ready and prepared to meet his doom.

The coyote stumbled as he tried to leap—once, twice. Bird Singer drew his sling. He loaded the weapon with the sky stone, and by the time the animal sprang, his missile was in the air.

The silver talisman flashed in the morning sun like a lightening bolt as it struck the coyote's head. The animal fell at the warrior's feet. It trembled for a moment, and then lay still.

The Apache kneeled beside the coyote. He reached out to touch the animal that had almost taken his life, but his hand changed course before his fingers brushed against the creature's fur. Instead he grasped the glittering object beside the dead predator.

The warrior stood holding Bird Singer's talisman in his outstretched hand. There was no malice in his eyes as he approached the shaman.

The Apache spoke a single word when he placed the sky stone into Bird Singer's hand. He said the word again as he walked away.

The holy man returned Spider Woman's gift to his amulet bag. He understood almost nothing of Apache language. But he understood this: his people would have no trouble with these raiders.

John T. Biggs

Everything John T. Biggs writes is so full of Oklahoma that once you read it, you'll never get the red dirt stains washed out of your mind. The tribes play a significant role. No authentic discussion of the state is possible without them. Traditional Native American legends are reworked and set in the modern era, the way oral historians always intended.

Born in Herrin, Illinois, John fell in love with Oklahoma when looking for a job. It was nothing like the movies had led him to expect. The dust bowl was over. Cowboy hats were as popular as ever. Horses too, but people mostly rode around in cars or pickup trucks when they had serious traveling to do. Oklahoma had a diverse population, and he knew he'd have to write about it sooner or later.

One of John's stories, "Boy Witch" took grand prize in the 80th annual Writer's Digest Competition in 2011. Another won third prize in the 2011 Lorian Hemingway short story contest. He's had over sixty short stories published in one form, and four novels: *Owl Dreams*, *Popsicle Styx*, *Sacred Alarm Clock*, and *Cherokee Ice*. The opening novel of his first series, *Clementine*, will be released this summer.

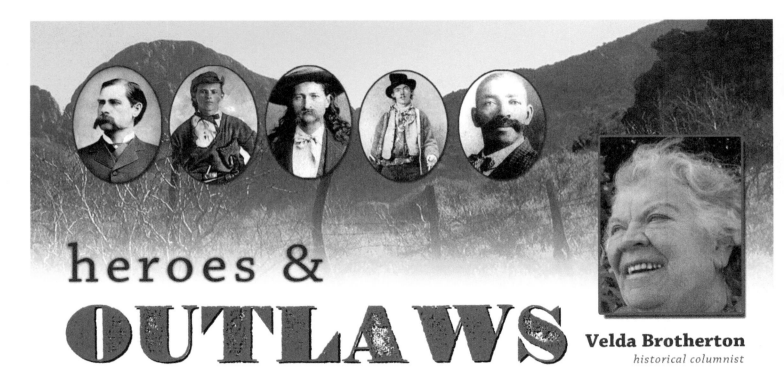

heroes &
OUTLAWS

Velda Brotherton
historical columnist

Fort Smith began as a small stockade fort in 1817. The first US Marshal appointed in the district was George Washington Scott, May, 1820. For a complete list of US Marshals serving the Western Arkansas District, Google *Western District of Arkansas History*.

The first fort burned, and another was built. It remained on the western frontier long after the Civil War. Across the river lay Indian Territory where no white man's law applied. In 1871 the military abandoned the fort, and in 1872 the Federal Court for the Western District of Arkansas moved in. In 1875 Judge Isaac C. Parker was appointed to serve in the Western District Court. The geographical area over which he would reign was vast and untamed. His jurisdiction included seventeen counties in east and northeast Arkansas, thirteen counties in the west and northwest part of the state, plus the Indian Territory. The area under his watch contained approximately 74,000 square miles of some of the wildest country in any judicial court. And there the marshals rode herd on hundreds of outlaws wanted for murder and mayhem.

It is not true, as has been published more than once, that the appointment of Parker by President U.S. Grant gave him judicial power unequaled in the annals of American law. It *is* true, however, that the man did possess *a lot* of power—much of it due to the the the structure of his court, rather than the size.

Within the Fort Smith court, the federal district court and the federal circuit court were combined. Unusual, because the federal circuit court was the appellate court, which heard appeals to sentences handed down in the federal district court. Judge Parker heard cases in both of them, so when he sentenced a man to die and it was appealed, he decided if his own sentence was valid.

It wasn't until May of 1889 that Congress provided appeals to the Supreme Court of the United States for criminal cases. However, those sentenced by Parker did have another recourse besides being heard by the same judge who had originally sentenced them. They could take it to the president himself. It's noted, however, that the president was reluctant to override judgment of the man he had appointed.

So it would seem that Parker pretty much ruled supreme in the criminal justice system of the Western Fort Smith District Court. In two instances, however, Parker heard appeals on cases in Circuit Court and granted them not only new trials, but later discharged the two men originally charged with murder. Both were Indians who had been convicted of murder.

In 1885 Parker and Defense Attorney Sandels recommended the commutation of the death penalty in the case of three young Creek boys, citing their youth and ignorance. There were other rare instances when a death sentence—hanging in that day and time—were commuted. In 1884 Fannie Echols, the first woman sentenced to die on the gallows, had her sentence changed to life imprisonment by the President. Mat Music, a convicted rapist, received an unconditional pardon from President Arthur and Dan Jones, another felon sentenced to hang, received a life sentence. So Judge Parker wasn't quite the tyrant history has made him out to be.

The first fourteen years during which he served ninety-three men were convicted of murder and rape, and ninety-two of these were sentenced to hang. Must be where Isaac earned his reputation as the Hanging Judge. Forty of these were commuted by the President, and two missed the rope by appealing to Parker. In all forty-six of the original ninety-three were actually hanged.

Parker did not go out on the streets and arrest these men. He did not ride through heat and cold, through rain and sleet and snow, through wind and the hail of bullets under the threat of death, into the remote badlands of Indian Territory, where most outlaws fled, to arrest these men he later sentenced.

Judge Issac Parker's Courthouse, which still stands today as part of the National Historic Monument in downtown Fort Smith, Arkansas.

Who did? U.S. Marshals, that's who. In the book The History of Fort Smith, Fred Patton writes, "The opening of the railroads in Indian Territory was followed by a horde of desperate criminals who terrified the country by their bloody crimes."

These guys were fearless and they'd banded together to take down any lawman foolish enough to come after them. Only one court held jurisdiction over them, and it wasn't the courts of the tribes residing in Indian Territory. Only the federal court in Fort Smith could see they paid for their crimes by sending marshals out to bring them in.

Parker once wrote, "For many years it was the ruffians of this immense tract of 74,000 square miles, extending to the Colorado line, that I had to cope. Criminals were brought to Fort Smith... they were brutes, or demons rather in human form." And he often said he could not have done it without the US Marshal's Service.

In Parker's court alone 103 deputy marshals were murdered in the discharge of their duty. Many others were deputized on the spot to take their place, to ride into danger, into the blazing guns of the hundreds of outlaws who felt no compunction in murdering lawmen.

In the twenty-one years Parker served, these brave marshals were responsible for bringing to the justice of Judge Isaac Parker's court 12,490 criminals. Of these, 9,454 were either convicted by a jury or they entered pleas of guilty. Judge Parker gained notoriety for having convicted and sentenced to the gallows more murderers than any other judge had ever done in that length of time. Because of the environment under which he and his marshals served, an environment never repeated during the days hanging was punishment for murder, it is probably an unfair judgment.

Many ancestors of those living here now have served time as a US Deputy Marshal. Some names can't be found on the record books, but considering the situation, where men were deputized on the spot, sent out to do their job, and possibly died, this is understandable.

The names of marshals appointed during Parker's reign are: James F. Fagan, D.P. Upham, Valentine Dell, Thomas Boles, John Carroll, Jacob Yoes, George J. Crump, and Solomon F. Stohl. This list does not by far begin to cover the hundreds of marshals who served during the lawless years on the wild frontier known as Fort Smith and Indian Territory. It's easy to understand why the decision was made to place a museum at the National Historic Site in Fort Smith to honor these brave men and women who served and continue to serve their country as US Deputy Marshals.

—*Velda Brotherton is an award-winning nonfiction author, novelist, and regular contributor to* Saddlebag Dispatches. *She lives in Winslow, Arkansas, where she writes everyday and talks at length with her cat.*

THE COCHETOPA *kid* — A SHORT STORY

PREDATOR BLACK

The cabin was colder than death. The crackling fire had fizzled out during the night, and Ma had not gotten up to stoke it. Jesse sat curled up in a chair, knobby knees pulled to his chin under a ratty quilt. Ma sat across from him with a buffalo robe draped across her lap, cradling a bundle of skin and bones in her arms.

The boy blinked at the gray light that filtered in through the frosted windowpanes. It had snowed again.

"Lizzy's dead," Ma said suddenly, not opening her eyes.

Jesse wiped a lock of white-blonde hair from his eyelashes and stared hard at his mother.

"When?" he croaked.

"What does it matter?" Ma replied, cracking open her eyes and fixing her gaze on the far wall.

Jesse let out a sigh and watched as his breath made a little cloud in the air. He glanced over at the wispy blond strands jutting out of the bundle Ma held. He envied the frail little body that was once his sister. Her troubles were over. She would never feel the pang of starvation and bitter cold again.

Without a word, Jesse unfolded his limbs, his cold joints creaking like an old Indian's. He stood up and shuffled across the floor to the oversized boots that had once belonged to Lizzy's pa, shoving his feet in as he reached for the coat hanging from the peg by the door. It had belonged to Lizzy's pa, too, and hung clear to his knees. The boy unlatched the door and stepped out onto the snow-covered porch. Cold as the cabin was, it was colder out here. He plodded to the end of the porch and whipped out his carrot, marking a snowdrift with a thin yellow stream of last night's broth. He jiggled it a bit, the last couple of drops hitting his boots.

The shovel had been kept by the front door all winter to clear a path to the creek and the outhouse—and the little barn, if needed, though the animals had been sold months before. He grabbed its handle and trudged upslope to where Lizzy's pa was buried. He pushed aside as much snow as he could with his boots and thrust the spade into the earth. The rocky soil was frozen but crumbly in places. He pried up several fist-sized stones and set them aside. Bit by bit, he chipped away at the frozen ground, widening the hole until it was large enough to hold a four-year-old. When it was as deep as he could manage, he trudged back to the cabin to get his ma.

"You take her," Ma said, holding out the little body to Jesse. "I'll watch from here."

He recoiled. He had never touched a dead person before. It wasn't the same as a dead bird or a rabbit. Ma stared hard at him. He choked back the bile threatening to climb his throat and held out his arms.

Lizzy was as light as a bundle of kindling and just as pokey. He turned and hurried up the slope as quickly as he could without appearing too anxious. When he reached the grave, it began to snow again. He set his sister's body in the ground, willing himself not to look at the wavy hair. He quickly wiped the sensation of death from his hands onto his overalls and shoveled the frozen crumbles of earth over the body. Snow fell in fat flakes, blanketing his coat in a soft, downy white. He worked quickly, piling the larger stones on top of the soil until

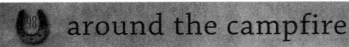

there was a little mound. The hole wasn't deep enough, but he hoped it would keep the animals away until he could dig a proper hole come spring.

He turned to face the cabin. Ma stood on the porch, arms folded under her shawl, a withered look on her face.

"Should we say something?" he called.

Ma stood for a moment, the tips of her stringy, light brown hair catching a few flakes that drifted under the porch roof.

"Ain't nothin' we can say to bring her back," she muttered and turned to go inside the cabin.

He stared after her for a few moments, then settled his gaze on his sister's grave. He cleared his throat.

"I'm sorry you died, Lizzy. I'm sorry we never had enough to eat." He shifted in place. "And I'm sorry I broke the leg off your doll. It really was me."

Jesse turned to go, then stoppped.

"I'll miss you," he said finally, a note of sadness in his voice, and he hurried back to the cabin.

He shook off his coat and knocked the snow from his boots before he set them by the door again. Ma was taking logs out of the wood box to start up the fire.

"I'll do that, Ma," he said.

"I'll do it," she said gruffly. "You get that meat cut up."

"Meat?" Jesse asked, bewildered.

He glanced at the table and saw some thin strips of what looked like rabbit meat piled on a plate.

"Where'd you get it?"

"The barn. Thought I heard someone pokin' around last night. You was asleep and so was—Lizzy." Ma choked back a sob and stirred the ashes. "Wasn't a man. It was a deer, but I never saw it, just the tracks. Went to check the barn and found a rabbit frozen to the ground. Wish it had been a deer. We could've used the venison." This time she couldn't fight back the tears.

He watched his ma's shoulders shake as she struggled to hold in her grief. Even at the tender age of eleven, he knew he should walk over and lay a hand on her shoulder to comfort her. But there had always been a coldness between them. Now and then he would catch his ma giving him a look that he was too young to understand. He could tell that something about him haunted her, but he had always been too afraid to ask why his mother hated him.

He turned his attention back to the meat strips, grabbed the knife from the sideboard, and started dicing them up to fry. His mouth watered, thinking of the good smells that would fill the cabin. They hadn't had any meat for about two weeks and had been living off the last of the cornmeal and flour and the few root vegetables they had left. A pang of guilt shot through him. It was the day his sister had died, and all he could think about was eating. She should have been here. Maybe if they had found the rabbit sooner, Lizzy wouldn't have starved to death.

Ma lit the fire and turned to look at him. "Put it in the pot when you're done and bring it to me."

He did as he was told and brought the pot to Ma to hang over the fire. He opened the cabin door and grabbed a handful of snow from the porch to wash his hands. It turned pink from the blood.

"How many biscuits we got left?" Ma asked.

Jesse knew without looking. "Three."

They had saved a biscuit apiece from the day before, though both Ma and Jesse had suspected that only two would wake up to eat them. They had been right.

He found himself wondering who would get Lizzy's biscuit. He was thin as a rail, nearly as bad off as Lizzy had been. Long, bony fingers stretched out from slender, skeletal arms. Light freckles peppered cheeks whose cheekbones protruded a little too much. Anyone with a good eye could just about make out the shape of the boy's skull beneath his skin.

The sizzle of frying rabbit filled his ears, and he looked anxiously at the pot on the fire. Ma lifted the lid and stirred the scrumptious bits. A heavenly smell escaped and filled the little cabin as the snow continued to fall outside. His stomach growled.

At last, the rabbit was cooked, and Ma set the kettle on the trivet at the table.

"Don't take too much," she ordered. "Got to save some for tonight."

He put a cold, hard biscuit on a plate and scooped some of the good rabbit meat next to it. He set it in Ma's place and spooned some onto a plate for himself. He glanced over at her. She looked old and tired and not sure if she wanted to live another day.

He reached for his fork, pierced a chunk of rabbit, and savored the greasy, juicy goodness as it passed across his tongue. It was all he could do not to wolf down every morsel.

"Ma, why don't you ever talk about my pa?" he wondered aloud.

Ma froze, and so did Jesse. He didn't know why he'd just said that. He set down his fork and swallowed hard as he waited for the cuff across the face that he knew would come.

Ma's fingers went white from gripping the utensils so hard. He could feel the anger rolling off her. She turned her fierce, brown eyes upon him and grabbed his wrist.

"I don't talk about the man that raped me," she growled, "not to the boy that looks just like him!"

She squeezed his wrist hard and flung it back at him.

A sour taste filled his mouth. He didn't know what rape was, but he knew enough to know his pa had hurt his ma somehow, and he looked like his pa. He felt a little relieved. He finally knew why his ma couldn't stand to look at him. He reminded her of his pa, of the man who'd hurt her.

He looked down at his food and suddenly felt ill. The warmth and goodness he had felt only moments before had been ripped away with one childish question. He licked his lips and drank some water, trying to wash the greasy taste from his mouth. He looked down at the meat. He hadn't noticed it before, but it didn't look much like rabbit meat. As a matter of fact, it didn't taste much like rabbit meat. What if the animal had been sick when it had died? He'd heard that animals could get sick with rabies. What if it had died of rabies? Would he and Ma get rabies, too?

He shot a glance at Ma. She sat there, seething and looking away from him. He leaned back in his chair and fiddled with a hunk of meat in his teeth. As he went over the events of the morning in his mind, something struck him as odd. He hadn't seen his ma's tracks or the deer's tracks in the snow.

"Of course ya didn't, fool boy. Snow covered 'em up," his ma retorted when he questioned her.

He looked down at his plate. He hadn't thought about the snow.

"Ma," he said, looking up at her suddenly, "did you save me the skin?"

"No."

"We always save the skin."

"Well, this time I didn't."

"What'd you do with it?"

Ma whipped her head around and faced Jesse. "I threw it in the snow."

"What about the bones?"

"I threw them, too. Now quit askin' such fool questions!"

He sat in silence for a moment. "You always save the bones," he mumbled.

"What?"

"You always save the bones," he said in a louder voice. "You use them in soup. I seen you."

She didn't respond.

Jesse swallowed hard as a horrible thought took root in his mind. "Ma, what did I bury in Lizzy's grave?"

Ma turned her whole body to face him fully, anger coursing through her eyes. "You buried your sister. What do you think you buried?"

The boy looked hard at his mother a moment. In an instant, he erupted from the table, knocking over his chair, and raced for the door. He flung himself outside in his stocking feet and plowed through the snow to Lizzy's grave. The cold bit through his overalls and shirt, but he didn't care.

He threw himself down in the snow by the fresh burial mound and clawed at the rocks and soil with his bare hands. Snow continued to fall until his pale hair was made even whiter with a layer of snowflakes.

At last, he reached the tattered blanket his sister's body had been wrapped in. He trembled. He forced himself to look at the blond strands poking out the end of the blanket. Shakily, he reached for the corner of the cloth and tried to pull it away from the corpse. He scowled. The blanket had been wrapped clean around her, and he'd have to lift her up to unwrap her. He gingerly lifted the stiff body out of the hole and

unwrapped another layer. He set her back in the ground. With trembling fingers, he reached out and peeled the blanket away from his sister's face.

It was Lizzy, all right, poor, sweet, dead Lizzy. He wondered if Ma had had time to put her in her best dress. He pulled away the rest of the blanket.

He screeched.

Blood was everywhere—on her arms, on her legs, and smeared across the part of the blanket that had been touching her limbs. His gaze settled on the pinkish white sticks she had been buried with.

In a moment of horror, he realized what those sticks were.

Lizzy's flesh had been carved away from her arms and legs, her skin peeled back to settle in loose folds. The sticks were her bones.

He panicked and sprang backward into a snowdrift. He scrambled away as quickly as he could—right into the frozen grave of Lizzy's pa. He let out a screech and flopped over on all fours, vomiting into the snow. He heaved and heaved until his face was wet with sick and nothing but foul-smelling air came up.

He rose to his feet and staggered a few steps before collapsing again. He had to get away from here. He would get away. He'd leave now. He got to his knees, scooped up a handful of snow, and washed the vomit from his face. His toes had started to hurt, and his nose was feeling the bite of the cold air. He couldn't leave without his boots and coat. He'd never survive. He'd have to return to the cabin and face her.

The door was standing wide open when he peered in. Ma hadn't moved and now sat with her elbows on the table, head buried in her hands. He stepped inside silently and tiptoed past her. He grabbed the knife from the sideboard and stood with the blade pointed at his mother. She didn't look up. He backed away, never taking his eyes off her, and grabbed a fresh pair of stockings. He shoved them in the coat pocket and slipped his feet into the boots. He flung the ratty quilt over his shoulder and turned to leave.

"Jesse..."

The boy's eyes flashed as he faced his mother.

"Don't say another word to me. You should be hanged for what you done—for what you made me do."

He turned to leave, pausing briefly at the door. Without turning to look at his ma, he said, "Don't come look for me. If you do, I'll kill you myself."

Without a glance back, he set out for the woods. He had wandered a quarter mile from the cabin when he heard the shot. He paused. A single tear swelled and spilled over his freckled cheek. He didn't cry for his ma, but for himself.

Jesse was alone, and he doubted he would survive the night.

• • •

The snow continued to fall until just past noon before it quit for the day. Jesse found an old game trail and followed it along the skirt of the mountain, plowing through the deep snow as best he could. He stopped once at a boulder to change his stockings. The snow that had clung to his first pair had melted inside his boots and threatened to freeze his toes. He spied a nearby bush with a few rose hips and plucked them from the branches. He split open each wrinkled pod and scooped out the seed fluff, popping the leathery skins into his mouth. They tasted tart and wonderful. He picked all that he could find and dropped them into his coat pocket. Scooping up a handful of snow, he shoved it into his mouth, allowing most of it to melt on his tongue before swallowing. He trudged on, stomach aching for a heartier meal.

As he made his way along the snow-covered trail, there would be a break in the trees every so often, and he could look down into the valley below. The Cochetopa River, black against the snow, snaked its way through the length of the valley and vanished behind a foothill in the distance. The faint wagon trail that led to the cabin was buried under a thick blanket of white. Ma had sold the team and the wagon late last summer after Lizzy's pa had died, and no one had ever come to check on them, so the trail would soon be nothing more than a memory.

He swallowed hard. No one would come, so no one would know he was missing. The coyotes and cougars would probably finish off Lizzy and his ma and scatter their bones, and if anyone they knew ever did come looking, they'd probably figure he'd met with the same end.

He didn't like it, but he couldn't keep the images of poor Lizzy out of his mind. Her skin peeled back like it was, flesh gone and bones exposed. He tried not to picture his ma lying on the floor in her own blood. He shook his hands, trying to rid himself of the sensation of cutting the meat.

He stopped cold. The knife! He'd grabbed the same knife he had used to cut the meat, probably the same knife his ma had used to cut away Lizzy's flesh.

He reached into the pocket of his oversized coat, grabbed the handle of the fixed-blade knife, and hurled it into the trees. A new wave of nausea overcame him, and he doubled over, vomiting up the rose hips. He sank to his knees and sobbed uncontrollably. It wasn't fair, none of it. It wasn't fair he didn't have a pa, and it wasn't fair Lizzy's pa had died. It wasn't right what his ma had done to Lizzy, what she had made him do. He couldn't set foot in that cabin again as long as he lived, and now he had no home and was going to die alone in the woods.

Why was this happening? Was he being punished because of what his pa had done to his ma? Was that why she went crazy and cut up Lizzy, because of what his pa had done to her?

A nearby juniper branch dropped its load of snow as a jackrabbit bounded out into the open. He looked up in time to see its large feet disappearing beneath a bush. If only he had the gun. And some matches. He could've had jackrabbit for supper and maybe lived through the night. But all he had was a lousy knife. The knife!

He sprang to his feet and struggled through the snow in the direction he thought he'd thrown it. Mounds of undisturbed snow filled the surrounding forest, but there was not a sign of the entry point where the knife had pierced the snow.

Panic started to set in.

He thrashed about in the drifts, fruitlessly searching in places where he knew the knife could not be. Breathing hard, he paused and closed his eyes, willing himself to calm down. He opened them again, took a shuddering breath, and retraced his steps back to the point of the game trail from which he'd launched it. He went over the moment in his mind, reenacting the exact muscle movements he had used to reach into his pocket and fling the blade. He had forgotten that a pine bough had moved after he had thrown it. The knife must have clipped a branch.

He headed for a snowdrift about fifteen feet to the right of where he had first searched. He approached the pine tree slowly in case the knife had bounced back toward him when it hit the branch. The snow was smooth except for the mound directly beneath the bough. Snow had fallen from the needles and caved in the drift where it had made contact. He doubted the knife was there, but figured it would be unwise not to check.

His fingers were already red from the cold, and he cursed himself for taking out the gloves Lizzy's pa had kept in the pockets. He fished out the wet stockings and yanked them over his hands like mittens. Digging down into the snow as far as he could, he rummaged through the cold, white powder, but there was no sign of the knife. It must have flown farther.

He stepped carefully from beneath the tree, taking one measured step at a time, scanning the white drifts for the slightest sign of a disturbance. At last, his gaze fell upon a soft blue shadow in a drift. It was about two feet long and narrow, as though something had dragged along the surface before sinking into the velvety blanket of white.

He kneeled and peered into the indentation. His eyes could follow the path the knife had taken through the snowdrift for a short ways before it curved downward. He carefully scraped away the top layer of snow, never losing sight in his mind of the path the knife had taken. Layer by layer he dug, clearing a larger hole than the one he had dug in the ground for Lizzy. Then, a few inches above the rocky ground, his stockinged hand rubbed up against the handle.

He pulled the blade from the snow and held it up. He was relieved to have found it. And disgusted that he needed it. Grimly, he wiped the snow from the blade and put the knife back in his pocket. He trudged back to the trail and picked up the ratty quilt. He stuffed the stockings in with the knife and reached into his other pocket for some rose hips.

Like it or not, he would have to harden himself against what had happened. What was done was done, and he couldn't change it. And if he wanted to live, he'd have to hunker down somewhere for the night and survive the cold. Then maybe he could think about making his way to a ranch somewhere and work for his keep.

The cold was seeping into his boots, so he plodded on. The game trail began to curve upward, but he didn't want to go any higher in elevation. He grudgingly chose to break from the trail and wove his way through the trees, angling toward the valley floor. There were large stones beneath the snow, and he stumbled every few steps, falling face first into the white madness on two occasions. The sky was gray, but as near as he could tell, the sun seemed to be hanging just above the far mountains. Darkness would soon drape its veil over the land.

The smell of smoke drifted his way and he paused, scanning the trees for signs of a fire. All he could see were branches and snow, so he made his way to a small clearing to get a better view of the sky. Just to the south, a small pillar of smoke rose into the air above the tree line. He stared at the thin, dark ribbon as it curled above the treetops and vanished into the gray of the evening sky.

Smoke meant people, which was what he needed. But what kind of people would be out here on this mountain at this time of day? They could be dangerous, outlaws maybe. They probably had guns. Why hadn't he grabbed the rifle instead of the dumb knife?

He debated with himself for several minutes before deciding he'd try to sneak up to see who had made the fire, maybe even listen to them talk if there was more than one person.

The shadows lengthened and took on a bruised hue as he gradually crept toward the source of the smoke. The trees grew in thick clumps with narrow rivers of snow running between them. He paused behind a cluster of junipers and squatted down to see if he could make out anything. The glow of a fire lit the ground near a fallen tree, but he couldn't see much more than that, so he moved to another little grove closer to the camp.

This time, he could make out the inviting orange and gold flames and the thin, dark column of smoke as it plumed and drifted above the treetops. A bearded man with a limp hobbled over and put a stick on the fire. A tall, thin man bent down and picked up a coffee pot, pouring the dark, steaming liquid into a cup.

His stomach rumbled. Where there was coffee, there was food. The tall man leaned over and stirred a pot next to the fire. It smelled like beans. He could hardly stand it any longer. He felt like bolting from the trees and grabbing the pot, but that would be foolish. The men would probably shoot him long before he reached their campfire.

The men dished up their plates and settled down for their evening meal. He scanned their camp for signs of others, but it seemed to be just the two of them. His stomach growled as the cold of early evening seeped into his boots. He couldn't stand there all night, freezing to death and lusting after their hot meal.

He decided to show himself. He reached into his pocket and wrapped his fingers around the knife's handle. He cautiously inched forward into the small clearing between his grove of trees and the log behind which the campfire crackled.

He stood in the snow while the men talked and ate. Neither one noticed him. It was getting darker by the second, and he stood outside the fire's circle of light, so he took a few steps closer, keeping a wary eye on the two men.

The man with the limp looked up suddenly and squinted in his direction.

Jesse froze.

"Bill, there's someone here!" he exclaimed, pointing at Jesse.

The tall man stood up and drew his pistol.

"Careful, Bill. It could be a claim jumper."

"Don't shoot!" Jesse squeaked.

The men glanced at one another.

"That sounded like a kid," the man with the limp said.

Bill kept his revolver aimed in Jesse's general direction. "How many are ya?"

"Just me."

"Come into the light where I can get a look at ya, nice and slow-like," Bill ordered.

The man with the limp set his plate down and reached for his rifle, laying it across his lap.

Jesse stepped through the deep snow until he reached the log.

"Stop right there," Bill said. "You got a gun?"

Jesse shook his head. "No. No, sir."

"What's in yer pocket?" Bill asked, nodding toward the pocket with the knife.

Jesse's fingers were still wrapped around the handle.

He considered lying, but he couldn't lie himself out of a dangerous situation like this. He decided to tell the truth.

"A knife," he said. "And a stocking."

"Show it to me."

He pulled the knife from his pocket and held it up, the blade catching the firelight.

"Anything else?"

"I got rose hips and another stocking and this quilt," Jesse replied, placing the old quilt across the log for them to see.

Satisfied, Bill put his pistol away, but left the holster open. He signaled for the other man to keep hold of his rifle and ordered Jesse to step over the log so they could get a good look at him.

"What're ya doing out here, boy? Ya lost or somethin'?"

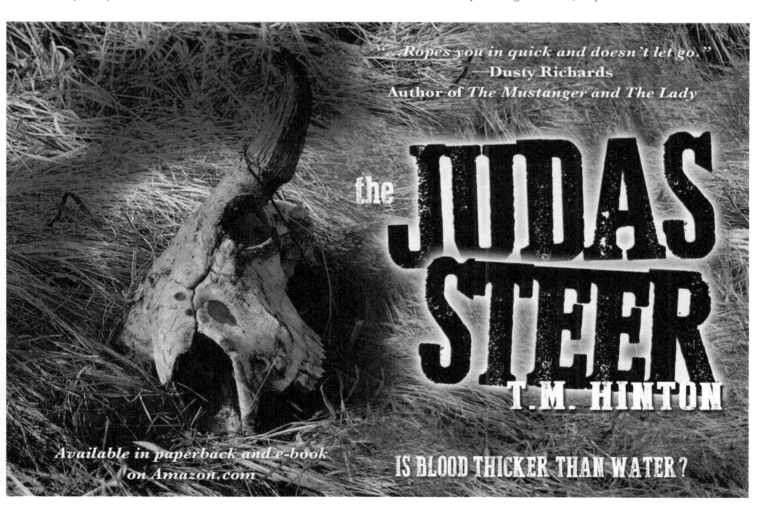

Jesse shook his head and reached his hands toward the fire to thaw out his fingers.

"Where's yer folks? Where's yer pa?" Bill asked.

"I never knew my pa."

"Where's yer ma?" Bill asked.

"She's—gone." He lowered his head. "And so's my sister."

The two men looked at one another and relaxed a little. He supposed they didn't consider him a threat, especially since he was cold and alone and skinny as a stick.

"You got a name, boy?"

"Jesse. Jesse Dixon."

"I'm Bill, and this here's my business partner, Randall."

The man with the limp nodded at Jesse.

"Business partner?" Jesse asked, confused.

"Go ahead, Bill. He ain't no claim jumper," Randall said.

Bill eyed Jesse one more time before speaking.

"Prospectin'. Pannin' for gold," he said, nodding to the small creek behind them.

Jesse hadn't noticed the babble of the freezing water above the crackle of the campfire. He looked past the men and into the darkness where he could just make out the black ribbon of rushing water against the snow. He wondered why they would be panning for gold in the dead of winter, but he didn't say as much.

"Think we're crazy being out here this time of year?" Randall asked, a smile playing at the corners of his lips.

Jesse grinned. "It's pretty cold to be looking for gold."

"Not when ya got gold fever, it ain't," Randall replied, chuckling at his own joke. "Naw, we hit some good color this fall, and just when we thought it'd run out, we hit another couple pockets. Just not willin' to wait till spring, I guess."

"Makes for some cold hands," Bill added.

Jesse nodded. He let his gaze rest on the pot of beans.

"Ya hungry, boy?" Bill asked.

He nodded. Bill drained his coffee cup in one long gulp and ladled it full of the beans. Jesse thought he saw a chunk of meat slip into the cup as the beans poured in. Bill handed him a spoon.

"Had anything to eat today?" he asked.

Jesse closed his eyes. He didn't want to think about what he'd eaten this morning.

"A few rose hips and some snow."

"Jesus, Bill. Look at him. The boy's near starved. Let's give him some of that hardtack, too."

Bill pulled a hard, dry square of cracker-like bread from a satchel and handed the cup of beans and hardtack to him. He shoveled a spoonful into his mouth and burned his tongue.

"Slow down, boy. You'll make yerself sick. Break that hardtack and dip it in yer beans. Let it soak a spell 'for ya try to eat it."

He obeyed, blowing on each spoonful before eating and savoring the good beans and ham as they filled his mouth and slid down his throat. He could taste that it was seasoned ham and made no fuss about eating it. He bit off pieces of the hard-tack as it softened and scraped the bottom of the cup for the last of the juice. Bill spooned another cupful of beans for him, and he ate more slowly this time, the frenzy of hunger having been driven out by the first helping.

Randall rubbed his bad leg and looked thoughtfully at Jesse. "Boy, if ya don't mind me askin'—what're ya doin' on this mountain at night and in the wintertime, no less?"

Jesse put down his cup and looked at Randall and then Bill. He lowered his eyes.

"We lived in a cabin over there a ways," he said, nodding his head toward the direction of home.

"That must be where the wagon tracks we saw this fall led to," Randall said to Bill. "We heard a shot this morning," he said, returning his attention to the boy. "Did that come from yer place?"

He swallowed hard, then nodded.

Bill glanced at Randall, then stared hard at the boy. "You said yer ma and yer sister are gone. They dead?"

He nodded again. "Lizzy died during the night. I buried her this morning."

"She sick?"

"Starved."

"And yer ma?" Bill prodded, but Jesse stayed silent. "Was she starvin', too?"

"Yes, sir. We all was."

Bill shifted uncomfortably. "Son, did you shoot yer ma?"

"What?"

"Did you shoot her—y'know—as a mercy killin', so she wouldn't starve to death?"

"No! I never! She did it herself. I couldn't—" His voice broke.

"It's all right, son," Randall said. "No one's accusin' ya of nothin'. It just happens time to time, that's all. Some folks'd rather take a bullet than watch their loved ones starve to death."

They sat in silence for a while, listening to the fire crackle as the flames danced over the logs. At last, Randall spoke up.

"Was ya there when it happened?"

"No," Jesse replied, "I'd already left."

Randall furrowed his brow. "You left before she shot herself?"

"Yes, sir."

"What made ya do that? Did yer ma tell ya to go?"

"No. She—she—" He buried his face in his hands. He sobbed freely in front of the two strangers as only a child could. When enough tears had been shed, he raised his head and looked at the men through watery eyes.

"What did she do, boy?" Randall asked in a kindly voice.

Jesse gulped and wiped his nose on his coat sleeve. "She—she cut up Lizzy and told me it was rabbit and we ate her!"

Predator Black

Imagine every Louis L'Amour western in existence lining the bookshelves in your childhood home as John Wayne films play over and over in your mind. The unmistakable slow clomp of your dad's cowboy boots echo in the little country store that is attached to your house, and you look up from the living room floor at the saloon doors that serve as the only barrier between you and the customers. His black cowboy hat appears first, followed by his sunbeaten face. When he swings through the batwing doors, you're looking at a man who stepped across space and time from the streets of some dusty Texas town.

Predator Black was thrown into the world of the Old West from birth, the sole offspring of a retired amateur bronc rider. After an abrupt move from Missouri to southern Colorado's San Luis Valley, the massive elk herds and abandoned gold mines of the Rocky Mountains offered new inspiration for the young writer—inspiration that only multiplied when the family moved to a bear-infested, mountaintop ghost town nearby. After a brief stretch in college on the east coast and a move back to Missouri, Black attended the annual Ozark Creative Writers conference where the first two chapters of *The Cochetopa Kid* took first prize.

shortgrass COUNTRY

John J. Dwyer
historical columnist

"This was a man."
—S. C. Gwynne

Quanah Parker was born in the Wichita Mountains near the present-day southwest Oklahoma town of Cache in 1848, nearly a generation before the War Between the States. He died in 1911, amidst a new world replete with Ford Model T automobiles, airplanes, telephones—of which he owned one of the first in western Oklahoma—and silent motion pictures, the first of which he appeared in.

Quanah arises as perhaps the quintessential archetype of the bridge from the old West to the new, even as both he and the West retained so much of their essential strength and so many of their distinctives. He was born into the most fearsome warrior tribe ever to rumble across the earth. The Comanches stopped the Spanish, the French, the Mexicans, the Apaches and numerous other tribes—and for a long time the Americans—from conquering the Southwest. His father was a legendary war chief and his mother an even more famous white woman. A member of one of the great Texas pioneer dynasties, she was captured by the tribe in a bloody raid, and then recaptured by Texas Rangers in a battle years later in which Quanah's father possibly fell in a shootout with future Texas governor Lawrence Sullivan "Sul" Ross.

His Quahadi band was the only North American tribal group never to sign a treaty. The loss or capture of parents, siblings, close friends, and at least one wife at the hand of the Texans and other Americans kindled a volcanic hate within Quanah. Through his mid-twenties, he himself killed Americans, Mexicans, and Indians from other tribes and participated in or led many raids and slaughters that involved robbery, rape, torture, and murder. The Comanches' victims included women, children, and even babies. These events stretched across vast tracts of land and many years. The Quahadis were the final Native group to surrender on the Southern Plains, and they did so in 1875 only when they were nearing starvation and relentlessly pursued by the greatest Indian fighter in American history, the dauntless Colonel Ranald Slidell MacKenzie.

Leader in Peace

While U.S. Army commander at Fort Sill in present-day southwest Oklahoma, Civil War hero Mackenzie dispatched Comanche peace emissaries to persuade Quanah and his few holdouts to come in to the fort, lay down their arms, and take up peaceable ways as American citizens. Surprisingly, those Native ambassadors found Quanah ready to surrender and urging his fellow remaining Quahadis to do so.

Upon getting to know Quanah, MacKenzie recognized in the fabled warrior a strength of character that spurred him to mentor the Comanche, teach him American social manners and customs, and guide him toward

The Meeting, *John Clymer's classic painting of Comanche Chief Quanah Parker greeting legendary Texas Ranger and cattle baron Charles Goodnight following the Plains Indian Wars near the tribal encampment on Goodnight's land. Quanah and the Comanches had once ruled the land and the two men had been mortal enemies, but would become lifelong friends. Courtesy National Museum of Wildlife Art, Jackson Hole, Wyoming (www.wildlifeart.org).*

leadership opportunities among both Indian and white societies. MacKenzie also persuaded Quanah's socially and politically prominent white Texas relatives—his mother's Parker forefathers founded the first Protestant church in Texas—to look past his bloody deeds and accept him.

After shielding the final Quahadi resistors from imprisonment in Fort Leavenworth, Quanah capitalized on MacKenzie's trust and influence. He also recognized the peaceful path of American citizenship as the best hope for his decimated tribe. (No more than three thousands Comanches remained alive at the time of their final surrender to MacKenzie.) As chronicled by S. C. Gwynne in his landmark work *Empire of the Summer Moon*, Quanah embraced and led them toward farming and ranching, attending American schools, getting involved in commercial business enterprises, participating in the civic arena, and learning the English language. Eventually, he founded an American-style school district for Comanche children that was owned and run by the tribe, and served as school board president. He also cultivated relationships with white leaders on the local, territorial, state, and national levels.

Quanah Parker – American

During the 1880s, Quanah parlayed his innate entrepreneurial and interpersonal skills and his burgeoning friendships with white cattlemen and business leaders, into a large ranch and a lucrative Comanche land-leasing business. He even charged his white colleagues fees for grazing and driving their cattle herds across the tribal reservation.

As his influence grew, some of those same friends sponsored him on trips to Washington, D.C. There, this former intrepid enemy of the United States advocated these and other enterprises that he believed were in the tribe's best interests before high federal officials, including President Theodore Roosevelt. He and Roosevelt developed a lasting friendship, as evinced by their famous 1905 wolf hunt near Frederick, Oklahoma Territory and Quanah's riding in Roosevelt's inaugural parade. According to Gwynne, Quanah also influenced his tribe to get away from the Ghost Dance cult that led the Sioux to disaster at Wounded Knee, South Dakota, in 1890.

He also defended his tribe as he verbally dueled with government commissioners leading the Dawes Act process of wresting Plains Indian lands away for individual allotments to

Oklahoma-born artist Michelle Noah drew on the influence of Kiowa Ledger Art for this original work, **Here, Build Jesus House!** *It depicts powerfully-built Comanche Chief Quanah Parker telling German-born Mennonite missionary pastor Henry Kohfeld, mounted behind another Comanche, that he may build "Jesus House" on the site of this post oak tree in rough Comanche reservation country near the present-day southwest Oklahoma town of Cache. From discouraging beginnings, the thriving Post Oak Mennonite Christian mission rose here among the Comanches. Post Oak continues its work in the twenty-first century (www.michellebnoah.com).*

tribal members and sale of the remainder to settlers. Quanah helped delay the process, particularly regarding the large Big Pasture region in southern Oklahoma Territory. This enabled the Comanches to lease that half-million-acre area for grazing for scores of thousands of dollars for years. By the time all the land was allotted, Quanah had personally secured better terms and more money for the tribe.

He accomplished all of this amidst continual opposition from other Comanche leaders who were often older and usually jealous of him, as well as from a white-dominated society that for generations had bitterly fought the Comanches and other Plains tribes in total war and retained much prejudice against them.

In 1890 Quanah accomplished two of his greatest feats. The U.S. government named him the first and only principal chief in Comanche history, a high station to which the tribe would later re-elect him. He also built the Star House, a renowned two-story, ten-room mansion near the Wichitas. It was a dwelling of which the wealthiest Oklahoma or Texas cattle baron would have been proud.

White and Indian guests alike filled the Star House's dining room with the twelve-foot ceiling. Many of them were well-known figures in American history books, including General Nelson Miles, Apache chief Geronimo, Kiowa chief Lone Wolf, Charles Goodnight, Samuel "Burk" Burnett, and President Theodore Roosevelt. White cooks and servants waited upon them and Quanah hired white teachers as well.

Quanah's generous nature had drawn the loyalty of others at least as far back as his successfully recruiting other Comanches for raiding parties he led. It grew more evident as he aged. He spent most of the small fortune he had accumulated feeding the hungry who streamed to him and the Star House, and helping other needy people, not all of them Natives. Gwynne poignantly wrote how tipis often clustered around the house—even though Quanah filled it with guests—and he and other family members slept outside in those tipis.

The legendary enemy and killer of Americans, Mexicans, and other tribes had two white sons-in-law and adopted and raised two white boys, not counting former white captive Herman Lehmann, who considered him his foster father and applied for Comanche membership.

Tragedy and Destiny

Quanah retained a durable streak of independence, as reflected in his multiple wives in which he sired twenty-four

Star House, *Michelle Noah's depiction of the sensational palace on the plains that Quanah Parker built in 1890 in present-day southwest Oklahoma. Ironically, the Comanche chief and successful entrepreneur lost nearly all the wealth that built the house by serving and giving to the many needy people--not all of them Natives--who came to stay in it (www.michellebnoah.com).*

children, his leadership in the peyote-based Native American religion, and his long coldness toward the Christian faith. Yet after his pride and joy, gifted eldest son Harold, fell gravely ill with tuberculosis in the mid- to late-1890s, he witnessed young German-born Mennonite missionary Henry Kohfeld's evangelistic message to his son. When Harold professed belief in Jesus Christ to the Mennonite, the great chief declared, "I see, I see now what I never could understand or grasp before." Harold soon died, but according to Quanah, his son spoke frequently in his final days about the scriptural teachings that Kohfeld had shared with him, and died happy that he had found God's love.

Marvin E. Kroeker, professor emeritus of history at East Central University in Ada, Oklahoma, and a member of the Oklahoma Historians Hall of Fame, recounted what happened after Harold's burial:

"Quanah asked the people to go back into the chapel. He stepped behind the pulpit, took the Bible in his hand, and addressed his fellow Comanches. He had been to Washington many times, he stated, and had met presidents and senators, but never had he heard anything as comforting or inspiring as what he heard from the Bible and 'this dear missionary

today.' He urged his people to come to the mission every Sunday and listen to God's word. Here was the way to the heavenly home. Harold had told him he loved Jesus and wanted to go home, and God had granted his wish . . . Then Quanah said a prayer and departed."

Quanah was now the one person with the power to keep Christian ministers from building churches on Comanche land or even preaching the Christian gospel to the tribe. But he was also the only individual with the power to give that permission, which he did in 1896 to the persistent Kohfeld. And thus began the conversion of the greatest warrior tribe in history to Christianity through the denomination most committed to being peacemakers in the history of the American Church. And thus also was born Post Oak, the first Mennonite mission ever to a foreign land—the Comanche reservation. Post Oak Mennonite Church continues to serve the Comanche people to this day, not far from Quanah's birthplace.

Whether or not Quanah Parker himself trusted in Christ for eternal salvation is known to God. Following the loss of his son Harold, he periodically attended Mennonite church services. One of his Quanah's own wives, To-pay, was among the first Comanche converts to Christianity. Another of his sons, White Parker, served the Comanches in and around Lawton for decades as a stalwart Methodist minister.

Legacy of a Man

Quanah died nearly broke due to his ceaseless and selfless sharing of his possessions with others, usually those of various races who had nothing with which to pay him back. He could not bear to see anyone hungry. And according to white Cache, Oklahoma storekeeper Robert Thomas, "He was always kind, never speaking ill of anyone."

Well-known Texas historian J. Evatts Haley wrote that near the end of Quanah's life, recruiters wooed young Comanche men to join the U.S. Army. This would have led at least some of them into the World War I trench warfare, mustard gas, machine gun massacres, and other horrors that killed, maimed, and psychologically scarred hundreds of thousands of Americans. The old warrior stepped in and stopped the recruiters, declaring the inconsistency of recruiting young men to fight and kill when the white missionaries taught that it was wrong to go to war.

Gwynne recounted how in the final months of his life, accompanied by his twelve-year-old son Gussie, Quanah spoke to an enormous crowd at the Texas State Fair in Dallas.

In memorably unpredictable Quanah Parker fashion, he sported a war bonnet, buckskins, and moccasins, yet what he said was this: "I used to be a bad man. Now I am a citizen of the United States. I pay taxes same as you people do. We are the same people."

Indeed we are, my fellow Americans.

• • •

This article is a variation on an excerpt from Volume 1 of John J. Dwyer's new Oklahoma History work **The Oklahomans: The Story of Oklahoma and Its People**. Volume 1 comes out this fall. It covers ancient times through Oklahoma Statehood and ends in 1910. It contains in depth information about Oklahoma's Old West heritage (www.johnjdwyer.com).

—John J. Dwyer is an author, longtime Adjunct Professor of History and Ethics at Southern Nazarene University, and a regular contributor to Saddlebag Dispatches. *He is former History Chair at a classical college preparatory school, newspaper publisher, and radio host. He lives with Grace his wife of 28 years, their daughter Katie, and their grandson Luke.*

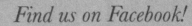

EUSTICE & CATS

a short story

richard PROSCH

Six miles away from the stagecoach line and Eustace Novacek, a man who liked living alone on the Nebraska frontier, still couldn't visit the privy in peace. He was used to the breeze whistling through the vertical cracks of the leaning frame outhouse, and he didn't mind the snow accumulating in the corners. But on a winter's night, when the wood smoke from his cabin got lost in the wind before it could cover the stink of the latrine below and the temperature dropped faster than his pants, he shouldn't have to share an evening constitutional with a needy, pestering varmint.

Again the white paw came under the door from outside.

Followed by a plaintive wail.

Then the paw through the moonlit crack.

Poke.

Poke.

He threw another corn cob at the doorjamb.

Damn cat.

He slumped down on the rough cut hole in the privy bench, canvas trousers around his ankles, tattered coyote fur shirt covering his chest.

The paw came again, trying to get his attention. And the meow.

Running short on cobs, he did his best to ignore it.

He hated cats.

Naturally, after he'd finished his business the cat was there, waiting for him with its breath coming in little frozen clouds, prancing around through the snow, threatening to trip him up when he trudged toward the house.

"G'wan! Get out of here," he told the fat gray tiger stripe.

He didn't waste his time kicking at the thing. Anything less than a lead pellet was useless. And God only knew where she came from. The way she hung around, and the size of her, made him think she was somebody's stray pet.

"Half a dozen miles from nowhere, in the middle of the Sandhills. You're a damned long way from home."

At the door, the cat shot between his legs, hoping to slip into the cabin. But he could move quick too, and slammed the door in her face.

The cat offered a complaining wail, but he ignored her.

He walked to his kitchen table, a thick slab of roughhewn oak and, sitting down, shuffled a deck of cards.

He'd been good at cards once. Good with a gun.

He eyed the big Colt in its dry leather holster hanging from a peg beside the door. Lately he'd been thinking about picking the gun up again. Maybe hit the Tuesday stage this month when it carried the payroll box. Then maybe retire to Texas like he always wanted. Like him and the Granger boys used to talk about.

Outside, the cat howled, but he didn't hear it.

He was too busy thinking about the heist, dreaming about his comeback.

• • •

After she caught a mouse in the hay barn and carried it to his steps, Eustace named the cat Yardbird and started to regularly share his supper scraps with her.

If you can't beat 'em, feed 'em.

But not too many scraps. Just enough to keep her around. Not so many she'd fall down on the job mousing.

He hated mice worse than cats.

One day, after a week of feeding Yardbird, he noticed she wasn't so fat anymore. In fact, she was rail thin. She must've had a litter of kittens. How many?

Standing in is open doorway, sipping a tin of coffee and warming his face with morning sun, he watched the cat trek across the muddy path to the barn. Every couple feet she'd stop and lift her paws, shaking off the mud with obvious irritation. One time she looked back at him in the cabin door as if he were to blame for her discomfort.

He shrugged, saluting her with his cup.

"Hay barn makes a good nursery," he said. Then he went back to the table where he planned his raid on the stagecoach.

It ought to be a simple thing. He and the Grangers used to be pretty good at this kind of job. And nobody expected a hold-up way out here.

He planned to rob the stage at ten o'clock the next morning. He spent a long time cleaning his gun and oiling up the holster. As time wore on, the temperature dropped, which actually suited him. Snow was the only thing stopped the stage, and when it got real cold it generally didn't snow.

He day-dreamed about how he'd wait at the Willow Creek curve. How he'd jump out in front of the coach, gun blazing fire. How his face would be masked, and his black Stetson pulled low.

Within twenty-four hours he'd be a rich man, ready to ride for Texas.

Which made him think he ought to check his horse.

Once outside, he found out the hay barn wasn't such a good nursery after all.

Just opposite the gelding's pen, he found Yardbird nesting in a pumpkin-sized hollow of musty hay. Without so much as a twitch at his sudden appearance, she looked up at him through amber-green eyes full of weary resignation,

Three balls of fur lay near her belly, one a tiger-striped short hair, one a darker gray, and finally, a still yellow runt seemingly cast off to the side. While Eustace watched them, the darker kittens wiggled and tugged at Yardbird's belly, but the yellow one didn't move.

Scrawny Yardbird might nurse two kittens. No way she had milk enough for three.

Before he could stop himself, he scooped up the yellow kitten. It wasn't dead... yet, so he carried it into the house. While he boiled water in a pan, he put the fur ball in an old pewter dish that used to belong to his ma.

He named the cat Buttercup. He didn't know spit about resurrecting a frozen cat, but something made him want to try.

It was a long night.

Buttercup was hardly bigger than a circus peanut and he was careful to be gentle. He ran warm water through the kitten's icy fur and gently stroked her fragile legs of bone.

At first she wouldn't take any of the canned milk he tried to feed her. But with patience and an eyedropper he found in his old warbag, she slowly came around.

By morning, Buttercup made a pathetic mewling, barely audible, but a good sign.

The sun rolled into the frigid sky. He yawned and checked his pocket watch.

Pert'near time to buckle on his gun, tie his mask to his neck, and get the gelding saddled up for the Willow Creek curve. Pert'near time for the robbery that would set him up for life.

But Buttercup wasn't out of the woods.

He chose to boil some more water.

And by the time he'd given Buttercup a warm bath and another few drops of milk, it was ten, and he missed the stage.

"There'll be other opportunities," he told himself.

But that night in bed, listening to the little runt mewl away, he wanted to toss Buttercup back outside.

Who knows how much was in that payroll box? How much had he lost on account of a stupid cat?

What a dummy he was.

"I'll get another chance."

And it turned out he was right.

Several weeks later, Jonah Butcher stopped by to jawbone and do some trading. Eustace let Jonah have a few tins of tomatoes and some cornmeal in exchange for a big stack of newspapers, a chicken, and a box of canned milk.

With Buttercup established as a permanent resident of the cabin, all three items were welcome.

That night he sat up reading while the kitten curled up in its fruit crate box beside the stove. A new bank had opened up nearby, and their hours were posted on page three. The ad boasted the brand name of the bank's vault.

He smiled. It was the kind of vault he'd broken into before.

Planning for a Sunday morning break-in, he carried his chicken bones out to the hay barn for the other cats.

By now, with warmer weather in the offing, Yardbird was more active and her two dark kittens had left the barn, following her to the cabin once or twice.

They were still wild and ran away if Eustace looked at them cross-eyed. So he looked at them cross-eyed quite a bit.

But it was good having them out there.

The mouse population was down, the gelding was more calm than ever before, and Eustace didn't feel so lonely.

Every night, while he dreamed of living the good life in Texas, Buttercup slept on the bed.

When Sunday morning came, Eustace was up before dawn.

While Buttercup roamed around the cabin playing with an old sock he'd given her for a toy, making various cat sounds, he checked his gun and strapped on his belt. After making sure the kitten had food and water, he locked the cabin door behind him and went to the hay barn to saddle up.

He and the horse weren't a hundred feet down the trail when he saw Yardbird and her two offspring trailing along behind.

"Get home," he yelled. "Go on!"

Ignoring him, they continued along the trail, sniffing at the spring grass, pouncing on a fly.

He figured they'd turn back once he outran 'em.

Spurring his horse down the road, he left the cats in a cloud of dust.

He shouldn't have stopped at the mile corner. He shouldn't have looked back.

Three dark specks were visible on the dusky morning road. In the clean, clear air, he could hear their meow.

What if they didn't turn back?

He figured there was little chance Yardbird would get lost. But what about her kittens? The black one had a touch of ringworm and seemed a little shaky the last couple days.

He looked up at the brightening sky.

What if a hungry hawk came along?

He planned to be back to the cabin before noon. He touched the gun in his holster. What if something happened to him?

He wasn't used to thinking about anybody else.

What would happen to Buttercup if he didn't get back?

Dammit.

Reluctantly, but knowing it was for the best, he turned back to the cabin. When he rode past Yardbird, she didn't act like she noticed him.

Little snob.

But she was right there when he got back to the hay barn.

• • •

Late that night, Eustace woke from a deep sleep.

The gelding was restless, and Buttercup wasn't on the bed.

Plenty of moonlight poured through the window. Chancing a peek outside from the safety of his bed, he couldn't see anything but the wide open hills with their familiar shadows.

The horse neighed again. Yardbird ran from the barn to the privy and back again.

Something had spooked them.

With Buttercup tearing up circles around the cook stove, he pulled on his trousers and took his Colt down from its peg. Quiet as he could, he crept outside, the Colt surprisingly shaky in his sweaty grip.

"Hold on," he told himself. "Hold on there."

What was wrong with him? Trembling like a kitten for no good reason. At this rate it was a good thing he hadn't tried robbing the bank.

Then he saw Yardbird back at the privy, crouched low, shoving her paw under the door, milking her claws on the old cedar wood.

He froze.

Somebody was inside.

As he worked to calm his breathing and stay still, a groan came from the other side of the outhouse door.

It was a low sound, a gurgling noise. Not necessarily a man. But what else?

Yardbird meowed and stitched a bounding path up and down around the little shack.

"C'mon out of there. Whoever you are, you're trespassing."

No answer.

Yardbird ran to him, circled around his legs.

"Don't you worry. I'm here."

Careful to keep his gun aimed straight at the outhouse door, he bent down and picked up the cat in his left arm. She purred and rubbed her ears against the buckle of his suspender.

Whoever their visitor was, he was being awful quiet.

Or awful cagey.

"Get on out here, or I'll come in after you."

The normal night noise of the hills abruptly stopped. No crickets. No spring peepers.

Silence.

Maybe he'd try again.

He let Yardbird jump to the ground, started to speak, and came face-to-face with an old friend as Dan Granger shoved his way through the privy door, a thundering six-gun in hand.

Eustace fell to the left, landing on his shoulder in a new-grown patch of thistle, while Dan stumbled forward pulling the trigger again and again, slamming shot after shot into the gray moonlit sod before landing on his face.

Eustace was up in a hurry, finger on the trigger, but it was already over.

Dan Granger was spent as his weapon, a lifeless husk collecting the settling dust.

Yardbird meowed with curiosity.

"I don't know. This here fella used to be my friend."

Yardbird answered like she understood.

She stayed with him as he turned the body over to face the sky with unseeing eyes.

Dan's shirt was soaked through with blood.

"Been shot."

But not by him.

"Meow," Yardbird said.

Eustace followed her into the privy where he found a sack full of money. Some paper. Some coin.

"That vault. The kind I used to know how to open. The kind Dan knew how to open too."

Yardbird answered him.

He nodded.

"You're right, girl Poor old Dan read the same paper I did."

He watched the cat twitch her tail and stroll back toward the barn, the night's excitement already forgotten.

Slowly but surely, the two dark kittens poked their heads out of the barn.

He looked back down at Dan. Poor devil must've been out of his mind with pain. On the run, probably didn't even know where he was. The Granger boys had the same Texas dream Eustace had.

And this is where it got Dan.

Before long, he heard the sound of approaching horses.

He opened the cabin door, let Buttercup run into his arms, then sat down on the ground beside the body.

He scratched the kitten's ears, and she purred in response.

Then she rolled over in his lap and let him pet her belly.

When the posse arrived, they'd find him here with his cats, the Texas dream waiting in the outhouse.

Where it probably always belonged.

Richard Prosch

After growing up on a Nebraska farm, Richard Prosch has worked as a professional writer and artist while in Wyoming, South Carolina, and Missouri. In the early 2000s, he won two South Carolina Press Awards and founded Lohman Hills Creative, LLC, with his wife, Gina.

Richard has written and published a multitude of short fiction, including three ongoing series of stories—*Holt County, John Coburn*, and *Jo Harper*. His western crime fiction captures the fleeting history and lonely frontier stories of his youth, where characters aren't always what they seem and the wind-burnt landscape is filled with swift, deadly danger.

In 2016, Richard won the Spur Award for short fiction presented by Western Writers of America for his short story, "The Scalper."

Richard and Gina live with their son, Wyatt, in Missouri. "Eustice and Cats" is his first story published with *Saddlebag Dispatches*.

let's talk WESTERNS

Terry Alexander
western culture columnist

Let's talk Westerns—Western bad guys, villains, those scoundrels who kill and defile the innocent and have evil intentions on the fair lady in the movie. Villains are critical in the movies. They must be vile, loathsome creatures with little or no redeeming social value. They must on first impression, overpower the hero and place his or her life in jeopardy. Some big name stars have played the Heavy. Who can forget Robert Duvall as Lucky Ned Pepper in the John Wayne version of *True Grit*? Remember the line, "I call that bold talk from a one-eyed fat man."? Clint Eastwood played a legitimate bad guy in the movie *Ambush at Cimarron Pass*. The movie starred Scott Brady and is one of the few times that Clint lost a fist fight in a movie.

In most of Clint Eastwood's westerns, he doesn't play a good guy in the true sense of the concept. In the three spaghetti westerns directed by Sergio Leone he portrayed a bounty hunter who killed outlaws by the wagon load. In *High Plains Drifter*, he was a killer and a rapist. In *Unforgiven*, he played a hired assassin. Not very wholesome, most of his characters have the thinnest edge of moral fiber over the people he opposes. The only westerns where he was actually a good guy are T*he Outlaw Josey Wales*, and *Hang 'Em High*, but that assertion is debatable. I'm a great fan of Clint's westerns, but he normally doesn't play the traditional good guy.

Everyone can come up with a top ten list of favorite bad guys and everyone's list would contain some of the same actors as mine with a few differences. Here are my top ten bad guys.

10. Robert Mitchum as the Reverend Jonathan Rudd in *5 Card Stud*. It's an interesting movie that co-stars Dean Martin and Inger Stevens. It starts out with a poker game and the lynching of a card cheat by Roddy McDowell. Everyone involved in the card game goes back to their usual lives with Martin's character leaving town and going to Denver, Colorado, until Yaphet Kotto and a series of murders brings him back to Rincon. Mitchum is very convincing as Rudd.

The secret is revealed near the three-quarter mark of the picture when he kills Roddy McDowell. This is a good western mystery with a great cast.

9. Walter Brennan in *My Darling Clementine*. This is an early movie version of the *Gunfight at the Ok Corral*, directed by John Ford and starring Henry Fonda as Wyatt Earp and Victor Mature as Doc Holiday. What is unique about this picture is that Brennan plays Newman Haynes Clanton, the father of Ike, who is evil and holds life in cheap regard. An interesting side note about this picture is that Doc Holiday dies in the gun battle.

8. Lee Van Cleef in *The Good, The Bad and The Ugly* as Angeleyes. The final movie in Sergio Leone's Dollar Trilogy also stars Clint Eastwood and Eli Wallach. The three men are searching for bags of gold buried by the Confederate Army and presumed lost after the Confederate detail assigned to protect the gold is killed. Angeleyes is a ruthless killer without any pity. In one scene he holds a pillow over an old man's face and shoots him three times in the face.

7. Eli Wallach as Calvera in *The Magnificent Seven*. He's the leader of a bloodthirsty band of outlaws. The Mexican and American authorities have driven the gang away from the heavily populated areas. To compensate they take the food and provisions of a small Mexican village. In desperation, the villagers hire seven men to drive the outlaw chief and his followers away. This movie has a great cast with Yul Brynner, Steve McQueen, Charles Bronson, Hortz Bucholtz, Robert Vaughn, James Coburn, and the guy everyone forgets, Brad Dexter. Wallach cemented himself as a first class heavy when he uttered the line "If God did not want them sheared, he wouldn't have made them sheep." Another good movie to watch for Eli playing a bad guy is How the West was Won. The only problem is he's only in the film for just slightly over thirty minutes. If he was in the entire movie, he'd have a second spot on this list.

6. Henry Fonda in *Once Upon a Time in the West*. From the opening scenes in which Fonda's character of Frank and his band of outlaws murder a family and walk up on the only survivor, you have the close-up of Fonda and look into his blue eyes. One of his gunmen asks, "What do we do with this one, Frank?" Fonda glances at the speaker, spits, and replies, "Now that you've called me by name." He draws his pistol and cocks the hammer, the scene dissolves to the train whistle and the town of Flagstone. He nails the role, but plays it in such a way that he garners a little sympathy at the end when he's killed in a shootout with Harmonica.

5. Bruce Dern is a good actor who has appeared in several movies and TV shows, usually as a bad guy. In *The Cowboys*, he has the distinction of shooting John Wayne's character Wil Andersen in the leg and elbow from behind and once in the belly before leaving him on the ground dying. His instructions to his henchmen: "Take everything but the fire." Bruce Dern said he received hate mail for years from the movie and others say that the movie damaged his career. It's interesting that in an earlier movie, *The War Wagon*, Bruce is killed by either John Wayne or Kirk Douglas. To my knowledge, he is the only actor to get killed in a John Wayne movie and kill the star in another.

4. **Dean Martin** in *Rough Night in Jericho*, the only time he played a villain, and he is a great villain. He plays Alex Flood, a former sheriff who tames the town and stays on after to take it over and run it his way. He takes a prisoner from the current sheriff played by Don Galloway and hangs him in the street. Throw George Peppard and John McIntire in the mix as a former sheriff and deputy coming to town to partner with Jean Simmons and run the local stagecoach line. Alex Flood's favorite line in the movie is "Whatever you do, always get fifty-one percent." Naturally Martin's and Peppard's characters are going to clash and when they do, the action is fast and furious.

3. Slim Pickens in *An Eye for An Eye*. This choice may surprise some people, but Pickens can really play a fearsome bad guy. In this movie, he plays Ike Slant, a man seeking revenge against Talion, a bounty hunter played by Robert Lansing. He rapes Tailon's wife, kills her and his son, and burns the house down around the bodies. Tailon rides off to seek revenge on Slant and meets Benny, a competing bounty hunter. When they catch up to Slant, Talion's gun-hand is injured and Benny is blinded. Together they come up with an interesting idea of Benny visualizing a clock in his head. After hours of practice, Talion can give him the time and Benny can put the bullet there. This is actually a B-western, but Pickens's villainy really sets this film on a different level.

2. Lee Marvin in *The Man that Shot Liberty Valance*. Lee Marvin was a Hollywood tough guy. He had a long history of playing western bad guys. Check out *Hangman's Knot* with

Randolph Scott, *The Commercheros* with John Wayne, or a later western, *The Spikes Gang*, with Gary Grimes and Ron Howard. But in this film, Lee Marvin sizzles as the villain, from the time he whips Jimmy Stewart with a riding quirt in the early scenes till the shootout in which it first appeared that he is killed by Jimmy Stewart. But that scene is a smokescreen and the truth is something entirely different. This John Ford classic is unique in western films. It has an all-star cast in John Wayne, Jimmy Stewart, Lee Marvin, and Vera Miles, and co-starred Edmond O'Brien, Andy Devine, Woody Strode, Strother Martin, and Lee Van Cleef. John Carradine even made a short cameo. John Wayne and Lee Marvin made three movies together. He is one of the few actors who has been killed onscreen twice by John Wayne. For those wanting to know the third film that Wayne and Marvin appeared in was *Donovan's Reef*.

This brings us to the top pick for western heavy. This guy had a long career both on TV and in movies. He's played the bad guy in several films, twice with John Wayne, and was one of the most believable actors in Hollywood.

1. Richard Boone as Cicero Grimes in *Hombre*. Made in 1957, this revisionist movie stars Paul Newman as John Russell, a white man raised on the Apache reservation in Arizona. He first runs afoul of Grimes at a stage station where Grimes tried to take his stage ticket and ends up taking Larry Ward's instead. Grimes and his gang, which includes David Canary and Cameron Mitchell, stop the stage and relieve Mr. Favor, played by Frederick March, a dishonest Indian agent, of ten thousand dollars that he stole from the reservation. John Russell gets the money back after a shootout with Canary and Mitchell, but the passengers have no horses and very little water and so begin the long trek across the desert. They arrive at an abandoned mine and stop to rest, only to be boxed in the Grimes gang. I'm not going to give away any more of the movie except to say this about the final shootout between John Russell, Cicero Grimes, and a Mexican gunman played by Frank Silvero—the final line Boone utters in the film: "Well now, I wonder what Hell is gonna look like." I have to say this: Richard Boone was a first class actor and a great bad guy.

Put your own list together. I'm sure you'll have some differences. If I were to extend my list, I'd have to consider Richard Widmark for *The Law and Jake Wade*, in which he played against Robert Taylor (not the one who stars in *Longmire*). Western movies are a part of film history. Some of the ones based on actual events have very little to do with the events they portray. Like any other media, they should be taken for what they are: entertainment.

—Terry Alexander is a western, science fiction and horror writer with many publishing credits to his name. He and his wife, Phyllis, live on a small farm near Porum, Oklahoma

best of the
WEST

Rod Miller
western columnist

It seemed to the young Englishman that if anyone had been watching from the bench he would have seen them like a print of Life on the Western Plains….

So begins the "Best" Western short story, "Genesis" by Wallace Stegner. Those are the thoughts of the tale's central character, Lionel "Rusty" Cullen, a 19-year-old Englishman who migrated to the cattle country of Saskatchewan in search of adventure. His musing reveals that by 1906, when the story is set, dime novels and Western art had already romanticized the Old West and made the cowboy a mythical figure. For Rusty, and the reader, this story corrects those notions.

"Genesis" is tucked into the memoir of the author's childhood days in Eastend, Saskatchewan, *Wolf Willow*. Born in 1909, Stegner said he "lived in twenty places in eight states and Canada," including Eastend, Great Falls, Montana (where he mowed Charles M. Russell's lawn), and Salt Lake City, Utah. He won the Pulitzer Prize for Fiction, the National Book Award, and three O. Henry Awards for short fiction. Stegner died in 1993.

But, back to "Genesis." Rusty soon realizes his romantic notions of cowboy life were misguided.

Already, within a day, Rusty felt how circumstances had hardened, how what had been an adventure revealed itself as a job.

Rusty also sees he is least among the nine men who ride out on a late fall roundup to bring in calves for winter feeding. Still, he is determined to prove himself a man among men.

He had the feeling that there would be a test of some sort, that he would enter manhood—or cowboyhood, manhood in Saskatchewan terms—as one would enter a house. For the moment he was a tenderfoot, a greenhorn, on probation, under scrutiny."

As in many Western tales, the land is also a character.

When he chopped through the river's inch of ice and watched the water well up and overflow the hole it seemed like some dark force from the ancient heart of the earth that could at any time rise around them silently and obliterate their little human noises and tracks and restore the plain to its emptiness again.

Weather, too, is a character in the story and the source of the punishment. The roundup is interrupted repeatedly by snowstorms; early blizzards that scatter the cattle time and again.

The darkness was full of snow pebbles hard and stinging as shot, whether falling or only drifting they couldn't tell, that beat their eyes shut and melted in their beards and froze again.

Eventually, the storms become so violent and the cold so brutal the men are forced to abandon the herd, even the remuda, to stumble across the plains trying to outrun death itself.

He does not need to be told that what moves them now is not caution, not good judgment, not anything over which they have any control, but desperation.

Romantic notions are further disabused by the awareness that these men, and others like them throughout the West's cattle country, put their lives at peril…

…For owners off in Aberdeen or Toronto or Calgary or Butte who would never come out themselves and risk what they demanded of any cowboy for twenty dollars a month and found.

As much as I like "Genesis" for what it includes—a realistic look at cowboy life and work in extreme circumstances—I like it for what it does not include. There's not a single gunfight. No Hollywood walk-down quick-draw contest, no bad guys shooting up the streets of a wooden town. There's no damsel in distress—unless you count mother cows and heifer calves. No horses racing at top speed across page after page with nary a stop for a blow, a sip of water, a mouthful of grass. And there are no six-foot-tall bulletproof heroes with broad shoulders, narrow hips, and a steely gaze.

That's not to say there's no courage, bravery, or heroics in "Genesis." But it's realistic valor, not the over-the-top imaginary superhero stuff so common in Western stories. Near the end of the tale, Stegner says this about Rusty:

It was probably a step in the making of a cowhand when he learned that what would pass for heroics in a softer world was only chores around here.

And that observation alone makes it the *Best of the West.*

CPSIA information can be obtained
at www.ICGtesting.com
Printed in the USA
LVOW05s1011120317
526913LV00022B/178/P

9 781633 731592